Husbands and Wives Were Connected in The Past

How to Find and Marry Your Soulmate,
Raise Great Kids and Build a Strong Family

The Secrets of Good Marriages and Families

WILLIAM BODRI

Copyright © 2019 William Bodri.

All rights reserved. No part of this book may be used or reproduced in any manner whatsoever the without written permission of the publisher, except in cases of brief quotations in articles and reviews. For information write:

Top Shape Publishing LLC
1135 Terminal Way Suite 209
Reno, NV 89502

ISBN-13: 978-0-9998330-4-9

DEDICATION

To everyone seeking even better marriage karma by searching for their better half, raising great kids and developing a happy family life while maintaining a strong relationship with their spouse.

CONTENTS

	Acknowledgments	i
1	Marriage is a Past Life Connection	1
2	Happy, Satisfying Marriages are Due to Compatibility	17
3	Where, When and How to Look for Your Future Spouse	50
4	Predicting and Preventing Divorce	72
5	Begetting and Raising Children	106
6	How to Strengthen Family Unity	168

ACKNOWLEDGMENTS

My parents stayed happily married until the end of their lives, and demonstrated to me that a marriage could be loving and strong through thick and thin without any major fights or arguments. They set for me the example of "good marriage karma" and a happy family. This was even foretold by their karmic astrology reading of *Tieh Pan Shen Shu* introduced to me by my best friend, Lee Shu Mei. I owe this work, written with a bit of humor and provocation to make you think, to the influences of these three people and hope that any merit arising therefrom should pass on to them.

CHAPTER 1
MARRIAGE IS A PAST LIFE CONNECTION

Do you have marriage karma? Above the gate at the imperial shrine in Hangzhou China there was once a sign that read,

> Husbands and wives were connected in the past.
> Whether for good or bad those connections
>   never fail to meet again.
> Children are basically past debts.
> Some come to give and some come to collect.

Marriages are most often between individuals who were at one time connected in past lives, and who come together again from past causes. Whether these causes are for weal or woe does not prevent a couple's attraction for one another. They might possibly reunite for love, for joint advancement, to learn something from one another, to do something together, or to fulfill past debts and obligations. Good causes or bad causes, without causes a couple does not come together. Their meeting and attraction are experienced due to the force of former karma.

Children are also karmic debts. They either come to collect from parents or to pay them back. Whether seeking repayment or to make repayment, it is only on account of debt that children arrive. Every person in the family is there for a reason.

As Hart deFoew and Robert Svoboda wrote in *Light on Relationships: The Synastry of Indian Astrology*,

> A child who comes to you with a horoscope of destitution does so because your own destitution karmas have also ripened and are waiting for you to consume them. The child is as much an instrument of your karmic fulfillment as you are of its.
>
> Similarly, a child who comes to you destined to enjoy prosperity has come to you because you, too, are destined to enjoy some prosperity. If you do right by that child, your mutual prosperity may develop yet further. If you mistreat it, you will be garroting the goose that is ready to lay your own golden eggs. Students of the law of karma marvel at the elegant sort of neutrality that involves both parties, often unconsciously, in creating their own situations.[1]

---

[1] Hart deFoew and Robert Svoboda, *Light on Relationships: The Synastry of Indian Astrology*, (Samuel Weiser, York Beach: Maine, 2000), p. 171.

This also explains that children are a karmic inheritance, but we should first focus on their parents, the marriage partners.

In China there is a famous fortune telling method called *Tieh Pan Shen Shu* (*Tie Bang Sheng Xuan*), which is also known as "Iron Abacus Numerology" or "Iron Plate Divine Number" astrology. The internal computational methods of Chinese Iron Abacus astrology remain a secret because the computation technique is only passed down from master to pupil in a lineage that stretches back for generations. This form of fortune telling was so named because it involves using an abacus to calculate various numbers that index sentences in an ancient book, and those sentences spell out a person's fate in life. Once you have the number of a sentence, by reading that sentence you will discover a portion of an individual's secret fated fortune.

In *Tieh Pan Shen Shu*, there are 12,000 possible numbers computed by its secret algorithm that mathematically manipulates your birth time in a special way. Those numbers refer to sentences that are so amazingly accurate concerning the details of your life that they are said to be "divine" (spiritual) numbers that originate with Heaven.

Many events in a person's life are revealed through the numbered sentences of *Tieh Pan Shen Shu*, and they are so unfailing that the fate revealed by a *Tieh Pan Shen Shu* fortune is often said to be "cast in iron (metal)." Since the fortune is so amazingly, remarkably accurate, the numbers calculated through this technique are also termed "heavenly (spiritual or divine) mathematics." Thus we have the name "Iron Plate Divine Number" astrology or "Iron Abacus Numerology." I have had this technique done for me several times and can personally confirm that this special fortune telling system has revealed countless details of my life, and what was my future fortune and destiny at that time (which subsequently came true), but which the astrologer could not possibly have known!

This system of prediction is based upon securing your birth time, after which the master computes a series of forty or fifty numbers. Each of these numbers refer to sentences in a Chinese book that state the years your parents were born, whether they are still married or divorced, whether they are at that moment living or deceased, their status in society, their personalities and particular character traits, and even their occupations.

All sorts of things are revealed about your own birth situation too such as the number of your brothers and sisters and their birth years. The sentences also usually reveal your destined occupation, but remember that the sentences are written in ancient Chinese. What this means is that "You will be a chariot driver" must be interpreted as, "You will be a taxi driver" or "You will be a chauffeur" since those are the equivalents in today's world.

HUSBANDS AND WIVES WERE CONNECTED IN THE PAST

I once took a girlfriend for a reading and it correctly said that her father was a chef, and that her own occupation had to do with "ships, wind and waves." At that time she had just quit her job as a clerk at an ocean freight shipping company and had recently become distribution manager for Coca Cola, both of which accurately fit the description of ships (transportation), water and waves. We considered her shipping company job an exact hit of this description, but the ancient sentence also correctly specified her job at Coca Cola. Coca Cola, as a liquid drink containing lots of frothy bubbles, could definitely be symbolized by "wind and waves."

A *Tieh Pan Shen Shu* reading might tell you the number of your brothers and sisters and when they were born. Most of all, it usually reveals details about your marriage spouse. This includes the nature of the marital relationship for good or bad, the number of your future children, and all sorts of other very specific information. It might even tell you the name of your husband or wife, their occupation or where they came from.

Pikwah Fields, a Chinese woman who wrote the only other English language book on *Tieh Pan Shen Shu* other than my own books *Move Forward* and *White Fat Cow*, commented about the sentences that were indicated in her husband's reading, a Westerner. The sentences produced by *Tieh Pan Shen Shu* in her husband's reading, along with her explanations of their accuracy, ran as follows:

- "He and his wife were from different races." Richard [her husband] is a Jew and I am Chinese.
- "His wife was lucky enough to get out of a hell that was controlled by evils." *Tie Bang Shen Xuan* always used "evil" to denote Communism. I swam eight hours to Hong Kong from Mainland China during the Cultural Revolution. For me that was a dangerous trip to escape from a hell.
- "His wife has to take care of a cash box and prefers not to lose a penny." I was a bank teller right after I married Richard. I was supposed not to lose a penny from my cash box during those days.
- "His wife can use a pen that is made of iron (Tie) to write down good or bad events that happen on earth." Tie was the same word of Tie [Tieh] in *Tie Bang Sheng Xuan*. In this case it means definitely. It also said that "by throwing three coins his wife could foretell secrets that hide in heaven." So far I knew how to read horoscopes and how to set up Hexagrams.
- "His wife was a generous person who liked to help people." I tend to give advice to people and not shirk my responsibility if I believe that they deserve my help. My reasons for

writing this book could prove that Shao's comment was correct. I always believe that we should do something for our world besides making a living.[2]

As another example, my best friend Lee Shu Mei has a sentence that says her spiritual master would be named "Nan," and her spiritual teacher who played a significant role in her life was named Nan Huai-Chin. My own *Tieh Pan Shen Shu* reading says that individuals named "Lee" will be of great benefit to me, and Lee Shu Mei's family are my great friends while other Lee's have always seemed to be most helpful to me in life. I have not yet married, but my *Tieh Pan Shen Shu* reading tells about my wife's characteristics and the children I would have if I decided on this route.

Such things are not fated for you can always change them. A vasectomy, for instance, will prevent natural children (not adoptions) and thus change a fortune through prevention even if they were fated. Becoming a celibate monk or nun will also close off the doors to marriage too. You must remember that you can always go against your karmic fate in life to create a new fortune you desire, for you created the karma that is due to come to you in the first place. Thus you are free to change it. It is only a guiding

---

[2] Pikwah Pia Fields, *Why Life Events Are Predestined & How Our Universe Originated*, (Hunter College, New York, 2003), pp. 168-169.

force in your life.

As Swami Sivananda of Rishikesh once said, "You are the architect of your own fate. You are the master of your own destiny. You can do and undo things. You sow an action and reap a tendency. You sow a tendency and reap a habit. You sow a habit and reap your character. You sow your character and reap your destiny. Therefore destiny is your own creation. You can undo it if you like because destiny is a bundle of habits. *Purushartha* is self-exertion. *Purushartha* can give you anything. Change your habits, change the mode of thinking and you can conquer destiny."

Zen master Yungu also said, "You cannot deny that fate exists, but only ordinary people are bound to it. Destiny cannot bind those who practice great kindness or great wickedness. For those who cultivate great kindness, the virtues they accumulate from kind acts is so great they can alter their original destiny for the better. The merits accrued can actually change their destiny from suffering to happiness, poverty to prosperity, and short lives to longevity." Therefore there is always the hope that one can get married, even if fortune tellers had said this will not happen, if you perform enough merit to change yourself and your fortune for this life.

Other people have showed me their *Tieh Pan Shen Shu* readings within which the names of countries or islands they reside within are even mentioned. The fact that you can even compute someone's fate is because of the interdependence of all things in the universe, and the fact that sometimes the karmic laws of cause and effect that rule interrelationships can be codified and then determined through calculation.

Tieh Pan Shen Shu can therefore tell you the birth year of your spouse, whether you will be married once or more, the number of your children or even whether you will divorce. I have seen such information many times from inspecting quite a few readings. It can indicate many types of past karma you have earned, especially as regards family relationships.

Why is this all possible? Because ...

> Husbands and wives were connected in the past.
> Whether for good or bad those connections never fail to meet again.
> Children are basically past debts.
> Some come to give and some come to collect.

India has a similar fortune telling method called the *nadi granthas*. This Indian system has entire life readings written on ancient palm leaves, rather than in old books like the Chinese system, and these very fragile palm leaves are stored at certain private residences or in Hindu temples. The *nadi grantha* readings, when they are legitimate ones rather than fraudulent fakes sometimes being marketed, also specify information about your past and future although the future predictions are rarely as accurate as those of the past.

One major difference between the *nadi grantha* and *Tieh Pan Shen Shu* readings is that the Iron Abacus readings are mathematically computed in your presence, whereas the *nadi grantha* readings are already written down on ancient palm leaves that must be retrieved from a library.

It is a Hindu *nadi* reader's job to go and find the correct *nadi* leaf reading from their collection that corresponds to your birth time, which they determine from the information you give and by looking at your thumbprint. Sometimes it can take months to find the correct palm leaf *nadi* reading, or they may not even have it at all. Unfortunately, there are many *nadi granthas,* and not all of them are accurate. Therefore it takes a lot of research to find a genuine, accurate one. Furthermore, in many cases a temple doesn't have an individual's reading at all, but a *Tieh Pan Shen Shu* reading can always be calculated on the spot.

For another astrological system, the *Brighu Samhita* of ancient India, the Maharishi Brighu wrote down the horoscopes and detailed life fortunes (special events and ages) of countless individuals, perhaps 500,000 people. When an original *Brighu* leaf can be found that contains the correct horoscope of an individual, it not only contains details about their past, present and future but reveals the actual consulting day and time of the reading. As with *nadi granthas* and Iron Abacus sentence books, many people falsely claim to have an original *Brighu Samhita* but only possess fraudulent copies, with genuine versions scattered throughout India. A famous story of one individual who experienced the powerful accuracy of the *Brighu Samhita* runs,

> When he [K. M. Munshi] was in the city of Hoshiarpur he came across a Pandit who claimed to have an original Brighu Sanhita. The pandit referred to a particular page and started reading it. The first sentence on the page was "You would open this page on such and such a date (the date of [the] visit was mentioned)." "When you will start reading, you would be surrounded by such and such persons." The narration was absolutely true. The Panditjee went on reading. After sometime he read "When you come to this sentence, your secretary will remind you of an important appointment". The moment this reading was over, the secretary came out from a neighbouring room and reminded Mr. Munshi of his appointment with the Maharaja of Kashmir.[3]

Andrew Donovan, author of *The Naadi Palm Leaf Oracle of India,* reported on his own *nadi* reading which ran as follows:

---

[3] Samudrik Tilak and M. Katakkar, *Encyclopaedia of Palm and Palm Reading,* (UBSPD, New Delhi, 2010), pp. xxi-xxii.

The two dots on your thumb print are a first quality impression. This means you are knowledgeable and intelligent and progressing every year. ...

You are running 55 years.

You were supposed to come at this age and time to predict the future.

Your father is no more - his name is Timothy - he was in Defense. Your father was a very good man.

You had one brother, he is no more. You have no living brothers or sisters.

Your mother is alive - her name is Dorothy - God's blessings are on her. You have medical expenditure on her. She is dangerously ill at this moment, near death, but she will recover - to save her you must make a donation to your favorite charity. ...

You got married. You are divorced from your first wife.

Second marriage is still going on. Your wife's name is Angela.

You have been married for 11-12 years and life is going smoothly.

Your wife is a very good person with great talent, very good positive thinker, also well educated in creative work and is also doing writing work.

You have had a good education. You have a Degree in Arts, a Masters - some kind of architecture. You had your own business but have recently drastically changed your job. Now you do some kind of audio/video work and presently you are writing - this is a private job.

Your profile shows you are much more talented than you are showing presently. At times people are jealous of you. You are writing well - you will be very satisfied with your writing; here is promotion, money and sudden luck. You will have success and settle in business.

Your wife is your working partner; you will have no other partner - no outsiders.

You have changed homes in eight or nine months from now, locally - a very good change.

You will have medical money expenditures soon. Stomach operation. It will be all right. ...

In your last life you have done some sins, and in this life also - too many to talk about. You are carrying sins from your first marriage also, loads of them. You will have to do a prayer to make everything right for you. ...

In your last life you were born in a 'Kshatriya' family, people who were fighters. You were a warrior, a powerful man. Your name was Loaknat. You were in love with a Brahmin girl of the highest caste. You loved her but did not marry her, you left her and she cursed you - affecting your health. You then married another woman and had two children, but gave them pain and left them too. They cursed you as well - this is the reason why you can have no children now. These four people cursed you. ...

You had done all these things when you were middle-aged in your last life, but when you grew older you started doing very good work and helping poor people, which is why you have the good birth that you have now, this time. But you are still carrying your last life's curses, which is why you have had failure in your first marriage, no children, some health problems and no success in your mind and heart. We will give you the Remedy to clear them. ...

Later you will try adopting a child - again - and be successful. This child, a boy, will be very lucky for you. He and your wife will look after you well. ...

You will have name and fame. You will have a great following from the younger generation. Kids will follow your writing - you will write stories on the gods.[4]

---

[4] Andrew and Angela Donovan, *The Hidden Oracle of India*, (O Books, Washington, 2008), pp. 29-31.

HUSBANDS AND WIVES WERE CONNECTED IN THE PAST

Why can a *nadi* reading give such accurate information? Because karma exists, and some of the cause and effect relationships ruling karma have been discovered, codified into rules, and indexed in such a way that they can be determined through astrological computations. The methods for computing a *nadi* or *Tieh Pan Shen Shu* reading are kept secret, so most people must turn to ordinary astrologers (western, Chinese or Indian Jyotish) for indications of their marriage fortune, and astrologers must learn to do interpretations of natal birth charts, which are fallible.

Some of the karmic fortunes revealed by *nadis* or *Tieh Pan Shen Shu* are really just "high probabilities" rather than fixed events, which means they can be changed if you work at it. Others do seem to be fixed, or fated, which includes the family situation you are born into that cannot be changed since it has already happened, such as details about your parents.

The reading details, as regards marriage, often indicate partners from past lives who will meet once again. Their marriages were not "made in Heaven," but are simply a result of their own past karmas drawing a couple together again for whatever reasons that are the manifestation of karma. A husband and wife both have things to work out through their relationship, such as things to do together, karmic debts to be paid and lessons to be learned. Marriages are not made in Heaven but by ourselves, and however good our past life karma they still require work to run well.

Karma even explains why some people fall into love at first sight. One astrologer told me that one of his clients, a man, met a perfect stranger at a train station and they married one hour later. Even now, forty years later, the marriage was still strong and vibrant. Another of my friends once told me that she didn't ever want to get married but got engaged that very weekend at a party! Karma can be a strange thing.

Some of my friends have even said they dreamed about someone after meeting them where the dream showed that the other was to become their lifelong spouse, which happened. This too was only possible due to their having strong past life karma. Husbands, wives and children usually fall into these patterns of fated karma because …

> Husbands and wives were connected in the past.
> Whether for good or bad those connections never fail to meet again.
> Children are basically past debts.
> Some come to give back to you and some come to collect from you.

CHAPTER 2
HAPPY, SATISFYING MARRIAGES ARE DUE TO COMPATIBILITY

Today people get married for many reasons, and the majority of the time it is not due to love. For instance, in many countries the marriages are arranged by parents, and the couples don't even know each other before they wed. A large proportion of the world subscribes to this type of marital arrangement where perfect strangers start sharing the same bed and are expected to have children and make a home together. With such demands hoisted upon perfect strangers, the partners must first greet each other with respect and gradually become friends before their relationship can develop into love.

In some cases, marriages are voluntarily entered into as business or political partnerships so that both sides advance in society, which has also been a common type of marriage throughout the ages. European culture once saw this type of marriage common among the rich elites. In some marriages one individual is not interested in romantic love but in finding someone with wealth or status.

Love isn't entirely out of the question, however, for the majority of the world's people do want to marry for romantic love, but sometimes people fall out of love too. Love changes over time and can become deeper or deteriorate just as appearances can improve or fade as you get older. You might still love your partner after several years of marriage, but not "be in love" with them as you once were. That's why counselors sometimes hear, "I *love* him/her, but am not *in love* with him/her." How can you find a soulmate where this won't happen?

Marriages entered into because of the wrong reasons – such as because of the sexual desire of strong physical attraction for one another – are especially in danger of withering away if the lust diminishes because appearances fade. For instance, this often occurs when one partner gains excessive weight or stops taking care of themselves. Infidelity also sometimes occurs in a marriage, which is one of the sure ways to kill it, and a drop off in communication and connection between the spouses is almost always a contributing cause. In short, marriages entered into primarily due to sexual desire rarely succeed in the long run. Looks fade and sexual interest declines over time for everyone, which is why the partners must base their bonding on something stronger than sexual urges such as a deep spiritual commitment. Couples dating also need to learn that just because a boyfriend or girlfriend is exciting doesn't necessarily mean they'll make a good spouse for you. Excitement fades, long-term compatibility is the issue.

The key in all the many different types of marriage relationship possible is that they must start with respect and then build to deeper love. Then the relationship must be managed to retain that love; you have to work at a marriage to keep it strong. Acts of service for one another, words of affirmation, physical touch, quality time with the spouse and paying attention to one another are all necessities to help maintain the good health of a marriage.

Furthermore, to stay together for a long time couples must learn to master kindness and gentleness with each other. This involves how they talk and behave with one another. Couples have to learn how to be couples after they get married, and this will take some altering of their previous habit energies.

Basically, couples must *work at the marriage* to keep it. You cannot let other things, such as work, come before the relationship. Couples eventually get used to each other, regardless of each other's quirks, but to last couples must at the end, for whatever reason, arrive at compatibility, respect and friendship with one another. Few things come easy in life, so a couple must agree to work together to keep the marriage strong and vibrant. They have to develop what works into consistent regular habits to keep the relationship happy and strong.

The general rule for all the different types of

marriage in the world?

> Make marriage as good as you possibly can for as long as it lasts,
> For however long that will be.
> Do not create an enemy of your spouse who should be your best friend,
> But work on always maintaining friendship to the end.

Many years ago I once read that for a marriage to succeed the partners must work on developing five compatibilities with one another.

First, they had to develop sexual compatibility in the bedroom. Each partner wants something different in their sexual relationship and they must let their spouse know what they want without shame or embarrassment if they want it. They shouldn't be worried about what the neighbors might think either. Sexual desire can fade over time as surely will sexual frequency due to aging, but it is typically *at least* once per week in a healthy marriage, and usually more. Intimacy promotes a stronger connection between two people so couples who stay sexually intimate with one another and make sex a regular part of their relationship are more likely to stay together. Sex is an important part of a marriage (or similar close relationship) so don't live your entire life wishing that you had had more wonderful sex with your spouse, who is the very person you chose to have sex with as a lifelong partner. A successful couple needs to maintain emotional as well as physical intimacy for a strong marriage, so try to avoid the fate of the 20% of marriages today that are defined as sexless. Don't stop having sex. It is one of the pillars of marriage that separates a lover from a roommate. You must make and keep sex as a regular part of your relationship.

Second, a couple needs to develop greater communications compatibility other than just being friendly in their conversations. The two partners need to become best friends who regularly talk to each other in deep discussions of honest self-disclosure where they openly share their feelings and open up on all sorts of topics such as goals, fears and dreams of the future. Couples need to communicate with each other on deep personal topics where they reveal the core of who they are and what they really want. People get married because they want a connection and you make it here. They need to learn that their partner has needs, just like they do, and they need to factor both of their needs into the relationship. They need to develop a high degree of respect for one another while doing this and learn how to listen to each other to truly understand what the other is saying. They also need to talk though their issues rather than bottle them up inside. These are how trust, respect for one another and bonding all grow stronger. In their communications they need a degree of trust and respect to build a strong marriage. If a couple is not communicating then they aren't a couple and don't really have a marriage relationship.

Third, the couple should try to develop and share some degree of enjoyment or interest compatibility. This is where they enjoy some pleasant activities together and shared mutual interests such as entertainment, hobbies, travel or friendships. If you can share a hobby together then this is fantastic because whatever interests you share you should engage in together. These pleasant activities, shared jointly, contribute to a couple's mutual well-being and should be pursued for their own sake. In a marriage you work for the happiness of your spouse and the family as a unit, but it helps if there are some pleasant activities you naturally enjoy doing together. Couples who spend enjoyable time together tend to stay together, and it's about making the time rather than letting other things get in the way. Great couples, for instance, make their own couples-focused holidays or getaways even when there are children.

Fourth, in a lasting marriage the couple must demonstrate commitment compatibility where they share a vision of having something they want to *build together* – a shared future. The marriage should be based upon a common dream, vision or directional beacon both agree with that is the whole purpose of the marriage in the first place, otherwise why bother? The vision answers the question, "What do you want out of this? What is our bond of identity?" This could include the goal of building a family, participating in politics as a team, traveling together, or growing and developing together as soulmates who help one another, or even building wealth together and so on. The dream is something that betters their condition, something they want to strive cooperatively together to achieve where they can honestly say, "I'm better together with this person because I have the benefit of their companionship." As a couple the partners need a unity of purpose that strengthens the relationship over time while embodying an ideal of growth. Basically, you need to marry someone who shares your final vision of what is expected from the union.

Lastly, a couple needs to become financially compatible. If one partner is a saver and the other is a spender or piles up debt then the marriage is heading for trouble because the two will always be incompatible over the one issue that keeps them financially solvent. Regular financial disagreements commonly break relationships so a couple needs to learn how to match on money matters. They should both keep informed of their joint finances. Truthfully, money issues are at the root of an extremely large proportion of divorces. People often marry for wealth/income and they divorce over money issues as well. Therefore couples definitely need to regularly talk about their finances. One of the concerns is to prevent themselves from getting into financial stress because it is right on par with infidelity in causing divorces.

These five factors are important for a strong

marriage bond, and they involve the three important principles of communication, chemistry and compatibility. Putting it a different way, if communication, chemistry and compatibility are not strong within a relationship then separation is a likelihood. For instance, most experts polled will tell you that the number one predictor of divorce is differing values concerning sex, money, and children, which are the compatibility factors one, four and five aforementioned. This is why a couple needs to work on these five compatibilities. Another compatibility to match on is energy compatibility too.

For a really strong marriage the ideals and principles of the couple should be as close to one another as possible. Of course a couple doesn't have to agree on everything or always think the same way. However, they should share a common vision of what the marriage should be about and stand for, and what they want to build together through its existence.

The welfare of each partner in the relationship will only blossom if they consider themselves in a union, one for the other, and they work together at building their common vision. People know this, which is why they commonly long for a sense of soul connection with a spouse where the two can share some common dreams, values, and purposes for their lives. Deep inside, we all seek to *share* something with another who will be there with us until the end. Furthermore, everyone is looking for a partner who won't just help them shoulder the burdens of life but who will help them be a better person.

Research definitely shows that marriages are low-risk when the husband and wife view themselves as a team. On the other hand, marriages are prone to divorce when a couple is personality incompatible, which manifests when each spouse has greatly different views, values and communication styles than the other. For instance, a wife might typically press to discuss problems to solve them, but the husband's personality might be such that he normally dismisses her concerns or refuses to engage in a conversation and listen. This is an example of a common frictional difference that might build into a divorce.

Men, in particular, have a bigger problem than women in listening to their spouse. Sometimes they will emotionally disengage or get defensive during an uncomfortable situation, which can escalates matters, instead of calmly listening to complaints and then working on resolving issues. Men, as a general rule, need to learn how to accept low-intensity complaints (influence) from their partners, and in particular show they are listening to their partner's needs. By their words and deeds they must show that they are not brick walls but can be impacted or influenced by what their partner has to say. Then we have a true marriage relationship.

In one sense a lack of discussion between spouses can be viewed as a weakness in commitment rather than just a communication problem, for the truth of the matter is that if a couple wants to stay together they really have to work at it, especially as regards improving communication. "Working at it," which *proves the commitment of marriage*, means working through difficult issues together and changing your own behavior. It involves trying to solve problems with a calm kindness that also incorporates your partner's influence. For instance, discussing arguments calmly and *immediately after they happen* is one way that helps diffuse difficulties to reach new agreements, compromises and new understandings that will keep a marriage in the state of flourishing.

Couples devoted to each other need to learn to listen to each other and uncover any underlying concerns within their disagreements. Listening, which can solve problems, is how to deepen your spiritual connection to your spouse. Otherwise, perpetual arguments can lead to marriage gridlock where no headway is ever made over an issue and the partners feel permanently hurt and frustrated. Of helpful note, one marriage researcher found that the ability to stay physically calm during a marital conflict (argument) showed the biggest correlation with relationship happiness of anything he ever tested.

When couples argue frequently but this is balanced out by other positive interactions such as signs of kindness, affection or appreciation that remind your partner of your love – touching, smiling, paying complements, thanking the other, laughing together and so on – such couples tend to stick together for the long haul. Arguments are perfectly okay in marriages because when you perfectly avoid conflict all you do is store problems for the future because you never settle any disputes at all. However, you must approach disagreements with calmness because many marriages have been destroyed by one mean sentence spoken in the midst of the heat of an argument. Watch your words and speak with kindness. Also remember that you might always win marriage arguments but lose your marriage from always insisting you are right.

Several couples I know with highly successful marriages admitted that they sometimes get into heated arguments, but they had a firm rule to never go to bed angry. They agreed that if they could not resolve an argument they could always pick it up in the morning, but they would absolutely never bring anger into the bedroom. Furthermore, even in the midst of fights they tried to remember that the person in front of them was the person they loved just as was the case when they were young and arguing with their parents or siblings. They can fight or bicker with one another, but agreed that the love must not go away. Incidentally, famed marriage psychologist Dr. John Gottman said that you should always talk about a conflict with your partner afterwards in order to defuse the situation and reach compromise agreements or understandings wherever possible.

There are all sorts of reasons that couples are initially attracted to one another. Some women, for instance, are attracted to men who need them. Some like men that make them laugh. However, one of the most common complaints from men is that women seem to be predominantly looking for a wealthy marriage partner, and if they aren't rich or have high status they cannot attract the most attractive or personable women. Why? Those tend to be the most picky because their inner or outer beauty provides them with the most options.

A wealthy man can attract women, but one famous Chinese astrologer told me that in his experience with thousands of individuals he had discovered a consistent tendency. It was that very successful, wealthy businessmen have trouble living past age seventy because they put all their energies into business. Even though women want a family such men don't necessarily make good fathers either because they typically spend their time working and enjoying their money rather than their children. They usually spend money trying to purchase an education for their children rather than personally training them and teaching them the lessons they need to learn. They might be good at providing money for a family, but women need to understand the caveat that this doesn't necessarily translate into a good marriage or family. A "good provider" might not be good at anything else other than putting money on the table.

It is intriguing when women say that they are usually looking for the following characteristics in a man. They want him to be kind, gentle, loving and compassionate, a good father, and have a sense of humor that can make her laugh. However, when you ask a woman who is dating what her last boyfriend was like she will usually admit that he was nothing like this at all. For some reason what women want to buy and what they buy are totally different things.

Studies have found that women are often seeking "men with potential" and generally want the following characteristics in a mate according to roughly the following order of importance:

- Money, Riches or Wealth (great wealth and possessions imply a man can "support" you as a provider)
- Power and Influence (power implies that the man can "protect" you and provide "safety")
- Fame or Status (social status can provide and protect her and possible children)
- Good looks
- Exclusivity (royalty, hard to get, elite affiliations that imply "scarcity" or "a catch")
- Personality (humor, creativity, romance, mystique, intelligence).

Men know that women are usually evaluating them on this fitness scale, which reflects that fact that females tend to choose in a mate what appeals to them aesthetically as flamboyant splendor. In the human realm the equivalent is exactly money, power, fame and so forth. In nature males display to attract females which is why men joke that the most attractive outfit they can possibly wear around themselves to attract women is a $100,000 Mercedes Benz.

This is one of the reasons men pursue wealth other than just to live better. Money can get them hot women in the dating arena, and also a high class wife too. Alas, when men don't possess money or any of the top five qualities then they also joke that the only thing they can do is compete on personality.

Prejudices aside, it is a fact created from centuries of conditioning that masculine energy is aggressive but also socially centered around "providing and protecting" while feminine energy is more primarily focused on "caring and nurturing." Thus it is not unreasonable for a woman to look for a wealthy man who can protect her and provide. However, wealthy men are difficult to catch because money gives them more options. Males generally want a large *quantity* of sexual partners, meaning a portfolio of experiences that they can buy through money, while women prefer a *quality* partner, meaning a single but solid investment.

Both of the sexes have lists of things they want or don't want as general tendencies that even run across cultures. In general, men do not prefer women taller than themselves, older than themselves, more educated than themselves, or richer than themselves. They don't like women with an attitude who are "high maintenance." For most countries these tend to be common concerns.

A typical joke about unrealistic male expectations is a man seeking to meet a woman with model looks, a good education, who is smart but doesn't have an opinion, and who has money to spend but not a job so that she would be his follower rather than leader.

From her years of matchmaking experience Patti Stanger, the "Millionaire Matchmaker," wrote *Become Your Own Matchmaker* wherein she listed what highly eligible, rich men were typically looking for. What was the collection of traits they commonly sought? Happy vibrant women who smile, show joy in life, lack an attitude (are agreeable or easy to get along with), have long hair, are non-smokers, can cook, and who are not overweight. As to appearances, while men do indeed tend to look at a woman's breasts, buttocks and face, there is no one body type that all men adore despite the fact that they usually prefer woman whose waist lines are about 30% smaller than their hips.

Even so, men are visually oriented so tend to become attracted to another through their eyes. Women, being more emotional, tend to fall in love through their ears. They treasure what men say, and thus can be easily cheated by male bragging, promises, or lies. To be sure, men will tell lies or exaggerate when pursuing sex on the dating circuit. Many men, now in their later years, tell me that they deeply regret the things they said (or did) to women simply to get them into the bedroom knowing full well that they were not going to be marriage or even relationship material. Now that they are older they regret having cheated women. Women know many men simply want to bed them and a little bell usually rings in their head to protect them when they suspect a man is pursuing them for the wrong reasons.

Men and women have been pursuing consensual sexual relations just for the sake of sexual relations for millennium, and nothing will stop this. As previously stated, there are dozens of possible reasons for relationships and they are all equally valid, but they all have consequences that you must accept for that type of relationship. You have to accept accountability for the type of relationship you enter into. But consider this: if you are not always delighted to see the person you are thinking of dating, or wouldn't want to introduce them to your friends, colleagues or parents because of some type of embarrassment, then you should strike them off the list as potential long-term partner material. That hesitancy to introduce them to your friends and parents shows there is a problem.

Without a doubt, men pursue sex and are definitely attracted to appearances. As Patti Stanger once said, "the penis does the picking." Furthermore, "With men, it's all about the packaging – one look is all it takes for them to decide if you're a keeper or if you should be tossed back. This might be crude, but they're measuring your 'fuckability factor.'"

A famous comment related to this conversation comes from supermodel Jerry Hall, once married to Mick Jagger of the Rolling Stones. Jerry quoted her mom about relationships saying, "My mother said it was simple to keep a man. You must be a maid in the living room, a cook in the kitchen and a whore in the bedroom." There are all sorts of zingers like this that turn heads such as, "Women need to feel loved to have sex, but men need to have sex to feel loved" or "Men are like a microwave while women are like a slow cooker."

To tamper their expectations, women and men are often told that their significant other can be a husband/wife, lover or friend, but only one of these three and not all. The complaint is that you cannot find all three characteristics in one individual, so which one is most important to you?

For instance, can a woman who works full-time, or part-time, be a good homemaker? Or, can she handle the home as well but a full-time job makes her too tired to be a great lover? And what about the man … can he be a good husband *and* sexually exciting, or just a good provider confidant with whom you are compatible? No matter what the popular press states you can rarely have it all, which is just common sense and the reality of most people's experience.

I once asked a famous *Tieh Pan Shen Shu* reader in Asia what he had learned from his many years of computing people's fortunes and studying the results. He said, "No life is perfect. Someone can have great wealth, but a poor marriage. They might have a great marriage but very poor health. They might have great health and a fine marriage but no career success or terrible children. No one has everything perfect. You can never expect that. Furthermore, good fortune never lasts forever but bobs up and down. Trouble times are sure to come for everyone."

So marriages are this same way – none are perfect on all counts. They all have rough patches too. Even when looking for a spouse each partner has a certain "want list" of desired partner features in the areas of attractiveness, emotional chemistry, spirituality, intellectual traits and finances. Wish lists will never be perfectly fulfilled and you must accept this fact.

The Chinese therefore have a saying, "Seventy percent is good enough," and that's what you should remember in seeking a spouse because it will hold true even for your soulmate. Your karmic spouse will not be perfect. If, however, you have non-negotiable traits you desire in a spouse then you are advised not to become involved with potential others when it's obvious they don't fulfill the requirements, such as sharing the same religion. If you're not on the same page, why bother instigating false bonding when you don't want the same things? Don't waste your precious time with the wrong person, but move on. To hold onto a relationship with no future is bad for you and unfair to the other.

If compatibility is lacking in non-negotiable areas, if the other person isn't agreeable, don't even pursue a relationship that you already know is doomed to failure. One dating expert stated that you should decide whether or not the person you are dating is an "absolute not" within the first ninety days of dating (typically the Honeymoon period of infatuation), while one woman told me you usually know by the fifth bedroom encounter.

In the beginning of relationships you typically go through an infatuation phase (lasting from three to six months) and don't notice incompatibilities or brush them aside, but by the time of these benchmarks you should know what incompatibilities are there and problematical for a future relationship. There are different rules for when you should know you have no-deal incompatibilities, but the key principle is not to stay in a relationship where there are "red flag" or "deal breaker" incompatibilities to start because those situations just promise divorce. Despite the pain, end a relationship with people who are just not good for you. Don't get started with them, or don't go deeper with them. Walk away early. In addition to a romantic heart you must be thoughtful and wise about who, due to their characteristics, might truly qualify as a lifelong partner and parent of your children.

Additionally, you want to get out of relationships that won't blossom into marriage as soon as possible if it is marriage that you want. You tested it, it can't succeed in the long-term, so wish them well, move on and seek for that perfect karmic someone. Men tend to want to conquer as many women as possible but if you determine that a woman cannot be the partner spouse you want then don't get involved with her in the first place. When you're in love you want your partner to connect with all the important people in your life and when you're not sure or *know it's a short-term affair* then you want to limit those interactions.

Starting a sexual relationship when you already know that the relationship will lead to nothing will simply produce a ton of regret and bad feelings. There is nothing wrong with "testing," and there is nothing wrong with sexual relationships for that very purpose if both partners want this, but don't ever mislead the other and waste their time, taking them "off the market" during the most favorable years for finding someone who might truly become their lifelong partner. That's unfair to them.

One of the factors that both spouses especially desire is an attractive mate. Women tend to allow more leeway in this area, but men definitely tend to be more demanding. Across the world men seek attractive women as spouses or simply as sexual partners, but for a successful marriage a woman's appearance does not actually turn out to be the most important factor. Long-term the issues of compatibility, chemistry, communication, intimacy and values are what cement a relationship together – rather than appearances – and are what keep it going.

For instance, in Chinese culture there is a famous saying that runs, "An ugly wife is a treasure at home." While Chinese men are attracted to beautiful women just like men everywhere else, the common man knows he probably won't obtain a sexy beauty queen for a wife. He doesn't have a lot of money and there just aren't that many beauty queens out there. Therefore, the Chinese concept of marriage is more pragmatic than in the West. The Chinese man tends to seek a functional wife who will cook, take care of the home and care of the parents and children. He wants a partner who will help to raise the next generation well, and do it with him as a team.

In Chinese eyes a beautiful girl might also be a danger to marital bliss because she will usually be more demanding about income, might spend more money on clothing and cosmetics, and is more likely to be wooed away by other men. Facing these cultural views, a Chinese man can settle for a more functional spouse without complaint. In truth, your karmic soulmate is the most beautiful person in the world because of what is inside them and what they will do for you. It is the quality of the relationship that is important, not its outer appearance. Nonetheless, this doesn't mean that one or both partners should stop taking care of their appearance and health.

The Chinese marriage standards are more firmly based on companionship that entails harmonious compatibility (agreeableness), recognizing that the partner is one with whom they have deep "yuan fen" or karma from the past. Chinese husbands and wives tend to think of their mate in terms of pragmatic provider/nurturer relationships rather than in terms of romantic love or purely sexual attraction, which is more championed in the West. They don't just evaluate a person for their qualities in good times but evaluate their qualities as a spouse for when times will be rough and they will need to aid one another.

As previously stated, individuals enter into marriages for many reasons, many of which have nothing to do with romantic love, and yet all the reasons are equally as valid. For instance, some people get married simply because the culture says there is a need to do so. Who can say this is wrong, or that arranged marriages are wrong since they have been the norm in many societies for centuries and are still the norm in many countries today? Of course, matters do change over time. In India, for instance, it used to be that you would only marry someone from the same caste. Then the rule was relaxed to marry within your religion, next the country, and now simply a member of the opposite sex. Such modern attitudes took fifty years to develop and have overthrown the traditions of centuries.

Studies show that the happiest and unhappiest marriages are quite different from one another. The happiest couples know each other and speak as if in one voice because they know their partner's thinking, dreams and desires through and through. Like in *The Newlywed Game* on television, they can tell you how their partner will answer most questions because they know and understand them. If the compatibility is fine and their mind becomes one, you can say that they have become real life partners and true soulmates. These are great karmic marriages.

People with the happiest marriages are not out to

win over each other, but know the true value of their partner and aren't out to get them. They relinquish "being right" within the context of the relationship because it really doesn't matter who is right. Each is often the first to say "I'm sorry." Marriage to these couples is seen as a collaboration rather than competition. It is really beautiful music the couples make together. The couples avoid constant bickering and getting into destructive arguments because they really like each other and fear the danger of permanent damage, so they tread gently in dangerous areas. The partners also become focused on "we" rather than "me" and become cohesive because they view themselves as a team. They actually start using "we" language most of the time to show that their lives are intertwined as a couple. That's one of the signs of being in love.

On the other hand, the unhappiest couples have problems with compatibility synastry. When partners don't respect one another they must struggle to find positive things to say about their other, which is often the sign of a forthcoming divorce. In weak marriage bonds the couples will show less kindness to their partners, and there is a lot more disagreement and less friendship as well. Such couples rarely progress to a partnership of equals where both partners feel emotionally safe enough to intimately be themselves and value the other's point of view.

No one is perfectly compatible and there is no such thing as perfect chemistry even within soulmate marriages, so the key is for couples to view themselves as a team that wants to build something together and to actively work on materializing that vision. Couples usually come together not just out of love, but because of some joint mission, purpose or goal that helps to hold them together through ups and downs and when tempers fly and emotions rage. They must remember that this common vision is a stronger bond and commitment that unites them.

It is common for men and women to make requirement lists that expect the world of a partner (without putting equal demands on themselves) when the most important things are basically chemistry, compatibility, and communications. No one is perfect, including *you*, so remember the Chinese saying that "70% is good enough." Nevertheless you should definitely be stubborn about the important stuff. You are not perfect so you should not expect perfection in your significant other, but must learn how to live with another's flaws. Remember, for a strong marriage a couple needs to learn how to get along with each other, talk to one another constantly, forgive one another when things go astray, and live in general harmony.

How do you know if you are compatible with someone? To insure compatibility, the first principle is to *rule out spousal candidates* according to some age-old rules of incompatibility such as not getting hitched to a criminal, to someone chronically unemployed, or to an abusive individual. Never marry a partner either who has the major vices, addictions, obsessions or compulsions that typically cause divorce including alcohol abuse, drug abuse, gambling, and emotional, physical or verbal abuse! Stay away from deal breakers from the start and you won't have a deal that breaks.

According to the Edgar Cayce readings, divorce was warranted if any individual in a marriage was in danger of physical, mental or spiritual danger should they remain with their spouse, and "danger" includes abuse. If you are getting beaten up, are in danger of getting killed or your spouse blocks, disrupts or represses your spiritual practice or highest vision for life then there is no reason to stay together. If someone damages your values, life ideals and sense of direction, this is also a type of abuse to be avoided. Don't even think of getting hitched to those who have any of these tendencies.

The best way to avoid a bad marriage is to eliminate from consideration those partners with such problems in the first place! Many marriage counselors say that the *absolute best rule* is to simply rule out from the get-go those unqualified to marry because of these negative traits. For instance, the Indian sage Chanakaya advised that you should never marry a liar because they'll do that to you when first and foremost you want trust in a marriage. Another major problem is whether your potential mate is influenceable in the decision-making process. In other words, do they share power? If not, over 80% of marriages implode if this problem is present, such as one spouse trying to overly control the other. Since you can easily spot this problem of a controlling nature (and dismissiveness of your concerns) during the dating stage, you should be alert to avoid anyone with this problem as a potential marriage partner. You must be able to influence your spouse.

Furthermore, eliminate from consideration people with other detrimental, undesirable behaviors that you wouldn't even want as friends because they are too greedy, selfish, biased/opinionated, controlling, compulsive, overindulgent in spending or personal recreation, or not willing to help others. You wouldn't be able to stand such characteristics in a spouse either. Therefore, don't accept into your life anyone with deal breaker characteristics.

Incidentally, Edgar Cayce also said that divorce was fine when two people had worked out what was required to be worked out through their marriage – their karmic debts to one another were paid – and both had learned their lessons and were complete with one another. Cayce also said divorce was sometimes proper if one partner had overcome or learned their required lessons but the other refused to do so.

Behavior out of bounds – affairs, alcoholism, excessive debt, gambling and drug addictions, excessive pornography and violence or uncontrolled anger are very clear reasons that many marriages are destroyed. If you know your possible spouse has these issues or that they will probably develop them then do not get into that marriage in the first place no matter how much your heart tugs, for the subsequent suffering you will bear will probably cause divorce.

Don't get married just to get married but wait for the necessary compatibility, so remove from consideration those partners who exhibit the character traits that make most marriages failures. Don't fall into the romantic notion, "I can change my partner" or "my situation will be different." You won't be able to change your partner and your situation isn't different either. You need to know exactly what you want in a spouse because the person you love will probably not change. In fact, you should understand and *expect* that your partner-to-be will not change at all. And you? You're not going to change all that much personality and habit wise either just because you get married.

A healthy relationship isn't so much about a checklist of good qualities but about avoiding partners with harmful traits and personality types. *It's about avoiding the problem people.* Don't marry into a problem and you will avoid the usual misery that produces divorce. It is better to be single and free than burdened with misery.

No matter how much you love a partner, the truth of the matter is that a large proportion of marriages fail because of abuse that a partner cannot live with despite the love, so if a potential partner has any of these vices you should say to yourself, "Not

For Me" and move on to look for someone else. It has to be emphasized time and again that a secret to many good marriages is to have avoided the problem people in the first place. Life is too short and important to keep oneself in misery because of inalterable character traits you cannot stand, so don't ever kid yourself that you can change another person after marriage. Just say "pass" even though you might desperately want to become married, causing you to lower the bar of acceptability just so you can tie the knot.

The famous clairvoyant Edgar Cayce once said that each person in life had potential marriage compatibility with twenty-five to thirty other people, so don't settle for a stinker. Imagine that ... some people have thirty karmic possibilities rather than just one, which is perhaps why there is so much dating (or remarriage) going on.

Whom you ultimately choose for a mate depends upon your ideal of what you want to accomplish in the union. Don't make your life miserable just because you want to get married. Being a little bit discontent without marriage is a lot better than being absolutely miserable within a marriage. Don't settle into a shotgun wedding either just because you have an unplanned baby, as statistics show that this situation has a high-risk chance for divorce too.

I suggest three popular books you should read before getting married: *101 Questions to Ask Before You*

Get Engaged (H. Norman Wright), *The Hard Questions: 100 Essential Questions to Ask Before You Say "I Do"* (Susan Piver) and *Things I Wish I'd Known Before We Got Married* (Gary Chapman). The questions in these books, to be discussed with your intended other, will get at the root of what each of you expects of the marriage in terms of financial matters, raising children, the sexual appetites, professional goals, spirituality, where to live, and other issues of compatibility. You have to make your expectations clear before you get into what is expected to be a permanent union.

It is unfortunate that most people probably put more time and thought into buying a new car then they do in thinking about what they expect in the marriage with their potential spouse. Since a marriage means you're signing up to live with and have sex with only this person for the rest of your life, with whom you're going to share all your finances, you better get to the root of these issues before you tie the knot. Asking and knowing allows you both to approach marriage more realistically and actually serve the needs of your partner better.

When dating we tend to believe that the other person may be our future husband or wife before we get to truly know them. Too often we fall into a deep fantasy illusion of romance that must be brought back to reality. If we go over the issues raised within these books we can get a fair handle on compatibility issues before they rear their ugly head, and use that information to iron out some difficulties and decide whether the marriage should proceed or not.

There are also psychology books like *Men are From Mars, Women are from Venus, Love & Respect, His Needs Her Needs, The Five Love Languages, The Relationship Cure* and so forth that can help couples understand one another, but the most important thing is personal compatibility and communications with your potential partner. Since marriage is such an important aspect of a life, it pays to spend the time and money on a few books like this to try to understand the opposite sex.

Understanding how "Men are from Mars and Women are from Venus" can help you understand the psyche of the opposite sex just as *The Five Love Languages* can help you understand that everyone is different and your partner may express his/her love, or needs love, in a different way than you do. For some people this is a revolutionary understanding because they typically think that everyone mentally operates in the same way they do, but everyone ticks differently. Some express or want love through words of affirmation, quality time with the spouse, gifts, acts of service, or physical touch. If you want to maintain a good marriage you must express your love to your partner in the way that they most desire because that is how their mind is wired for experiencing contentment, satisfaction and well-being.

Most couples don't know that they didn't come together entirely by chance but by karma. In the dating field this is usually the case as well. People usually attract partners who are related to them from a past life, but who are also different than they are. Because your partner does things a different way, however, it doesn't mean they are ignoring you or that they are inattentive or uncaring. As *The Five Love Languages* explains, they just do things in a different way.

Vedic astrology (Indian Jyotish) and western astrology can often be used to gain an idea of the potential characteristics of your karmic spouse. This can be done by interpreting the 7th house of an astrological birth chart (the "natal chart"), which is also known as the relationship house, marriage house, or house of union. The 7th house reveals the characteristics of your marriage spouse and provides karmic details about your romantic relationships.

In Indian astrology, one can also produce a divisional chart for the marriage house, called a Navamsha chart. A divisional chart is created by splitting an astrological sign into a number of equal parts and then creating a new chart based on the divisions. In other words, divisional charts are formed by dividing the degree, minutes and seconds for the position of the planets within a natal chart into smaller and smaller divisions. For a Navamsha chart, which is used for revealing karmic facts about the spouse and married life, each sign of the birth (natal) chart is divided into nine parts to create a new chart according to the divisions.

If you don't have access to a *nadi grantha* or *Tieh Pan Shen Shu* reading, you can find out a lot about someone's marriage and spouse by looking at the 7th house of their natal chart together with the Navamsha chart. These provide indications of your karmic marriage relationship.

Western astrology excels at another method for gleaning information about potential marriage partners, which is a compatibility chart (synastry reading) that can determine whether a relationship is likely to be marriage material or not. In Western astrology a compatibility (synastry) reading foretells how individuals will get along with each other, and where frictions will usually lie.

For this type of analysis, the birth charts of two people are superimposed upon one another to see which planets fall in the houses of the partner making the inquiry, and from these relationships you can determine how potential partners will get along in life or differ from one another. This is excellent for spotting obvious conflicts that may destroy a relationship from the start. Oprah might recommend some question books for compatibility issues but this type of analysis can give some powerful insight too.

The Chinese have many ways to compare the compatibility of individuals, and the simplest is by matching their zodiac signs to determine their net compatibility. In western astrology the zodiac sign is determined by the month whereas in Chinese astrology it is determined by the year. There are twelve zodiacal animal signs in the Chinese calendar where people born in different years have a different animal sign that represents unique personality traits. To determine the compatibility of a couple you not only must compare the animals signs of their birth year but also of their birth month, day and hour as computed by the Chinese calendar. This requires special interpretation skills, and Chinese methods for comparing two birthdates can provide different insights on karmic compatibility issues.

In all of this you must remember that there is a natural compatibility between individuals or not due to their past life karma that is revealed through these factors, their natural chemistry together as individuals who haven't shared a past together, and the compatibility they work to build in their relationship. Marriages require work, especially work on resolving the conflicts that are inevitable in any relationship, so even with the most perfect soulmate spouse you should think of compatibility *as a process you have to work on* in order for it to stay solid and thrive.

In marriage you commit to a bond you want to grow stronger over time and commit to consistently strengthening it as it grows into an ideal shape you both desire. It's not about an intensity of love but about a consistency of regular effort and habits in building and maintaining a relationship through thick and thin, and for this to happen you have to find someone you don't just love but with whom you are highly compatible.

CHAPTER 3
WHERE, WHEN AND HOW TO LOOK FOR YOUR FUTURE SPOUSE

The question is often asked, "Where can I meet a good man/ woman who might marry me?" Women are told to frequent places where available men typically gather and woman are few such as auto and boat shows, wine tastings, investment conferences, adventure trips, industry events, cigar bars, hobby and fan conventions, political support groups, scuba diving venues, ski resorts, community courses that men normally attend and the typical bars/restaurants where men of wealth and power congregate after work. Best of all are charity events that cost money for a ticket. Yet another trick for young city women who can cook is to offer one-hour afterwork cooking lessons in their apartment for men, which usually produces quite a few dates.

Men are advised to frequent activities where women typically are found such as community acting, cooking and dance classes, political campaigns, volunteering efforts and other relevant venues.

HUSBANDS AND WIVES WERE CONNECTED IN THE PAST

Both sexes have turned to online dating to replace the matchmakers of the past, and there are ample courses and books to teach you how to write an attractive description of yourself, what type of pictures to post, and so on in order to prompt a response that might turn into dating or marriage. There are even speed dating venues that entail 4-minute dates with a line of men or women. Both sexes say that they can tell within 30 seconds whether they'd ever want to meet the other party again on a date. Typically men want the telephone numbers of about 70% of the woman, and the woman are interested in only 10% of the men.

As far as dating goes, astrology can sometimes provide indications as to the most auspicious timing for a successful partner search, and likely locations too (that usually involve moving very far eastwards or westwards rather than northwards or southwards). A marriage partner in astrology is usually indicated by the 7th house, and to find out what's romantically likely to happen in your life you must look at the seventh (or fourth and first) house, but using a *relocated natal chart* that is your birth chart recast for the new location where you have moved since birth. If you are living far from your birth location then astrology is far less accurate if you are not using a relocated natal chart. Astrological aspects to the "owner" or "lord" of the seventh house, and to house occupants or the house itself can foretell of positive romantic involvements.

TIMING

Sometimes astrological aspects are very helpful in indicating when you will have the best chances to meet someone significant in your life. In other words, planetary transits and progressions can alert you to auspicious timing for finding a boyfriend/girlfriend or spouse. However, if you don't seize the moment and make active efforts during those times then nothing will usually happen unless a new relationship "just falls in your lap." We all know that money rarely ever just drops into our lap, so during favorable times you should actively seek for a new boyfriend or girlfriend. Just as you must work hard to make money, you must similarly put some effort into looking for and then making a connection with someone who might become a boyfriend/girlfriend or significant other. You must put yourself out there and look at the right time and in the right places.

A bit of advice for women who see a man from a distance whom they are interested in. They are advised to catch his eyes and hold his gaze by smiling at him for five seconds without breaking contact. Then flip your hair and turn away. One matchmaker wrote that this is the most powerful form of flirting to elicit attention that women can ever do, and tells a man that you're interested in meeting him. Men can be a bit nervous in this area, so you must signal them of potential interest if you want to elicit a response.

They need to learn how to say to a woman, "Hi, my name is __. I [do or am known for x, y or z]. We haven't met before. What is your name?"

Men often have no clue about female signaling, so persuasion author Kevin Hogan offered the following advice about women's body language while mentioning that "men are body language idiots" in general. In an interview with Michael Senoff on HardtoFindSeminars.com he explained as follows:

"If you're a man and you're communicating with a woman, there are a few things that are typically misunderstood because there are such huge differences. So if you want to know if a woman likes you and if she's sort of leaning into your conversation with her hand under her chin, she probably is actually just bored to tears and this is the exact opposite of how men communicate with men. Men, if we're interested with each other, we might lean over the table and bend into the conversation and say, 'Oh, yes that's really interesting.' But women are the opposite. When they become interested they sit back and they say, 'Huh!' and then that's real. And women also tend to smile more than men, but we tend to get the wrong impression as men. We think, 'Oh, she's in love with me.' If she accidentally touches you, we tend to think she's in love. We believe these things are true.

"Women do a lot of things to be friendly on purpose or to be nice on purpose. They feel sorry for us, it's that maternal instinct. But when a woman moves into your space and she actually comes closer to you after you have been standing or sitting somewhere, or she gets up and goes to use the restroom and comes back to the table and then she positions herself in such a way that she's closer to you physically, now you know factually that this person likes you more. Women are very space-oriented, territorial creatures. So can you be absolutely positive? No, there are a few psychos left in the world, but generally speaking, if a woman moves into your space, and she's significantly closer than she was before, especially if she comes up, looks at you eye-to-eye 18 inches away or less, you can virtually guarantee that person has a very strong interest and it's not in business."

Now, as to astrological timing, the way to use it is to first find out which planet rules or owns your seventh house, which is the house of relationships. This is called the "lord of the seventh house." For instance, if the cusp of your 7th house is Leo then the planetary lord of your 7th house is the Sun. If the cusp is Cancer then the lord or house ruler is the Moon.

The Jyotish (Indian astrology) planetary lords are Mars for Aries, Venus for Taurus, Mercury for Gemini, Moon for Cancer, Sun for Leo, Mercury for Virgo, Venus for Libra, Mars for Scorpio, Jupiter for Sagittarius, Saturn for Capricorn, Saturn for Aquarius and Jupiter for Pisces. The western astrology planetary lords (which I prefer since they include Uranus, Neptune and Pluto) are Mars for Aries, Venus for Taurus, Mercury for Gemini, Moon for

Cancer, Sun for Leo, Mercury for Virgo, Venus for Libra, Pluto for Scorpio, Jupiter for Sagittarius, Saturn for Capricorn, Uranus for Aquarius and Neptune for Pisces.

Once you know your 7th house cusp sign by looking at your astrological birth (natal) chart, you can then determine the lord of the house. If you have moved to a new location then you should determine the cusp and 7th house lord for a chart that is drawn up as if you were born in that location, which is the relocated natal chart. The house lord can be well placed, well aspected, or severely afflicted, and an astrologer needs to tell you this information because it affects the character of your 7th house and is too complicated to teach in just a few words.

Now, whenever Jupiter or Venus makes a beneficial aspect to the planet that is your house lord then, other considerations aside, it is usually a good time to seek a partner. Secondary progressions are especially beneficial since they are strong and last a long time. In other words, whenever Jupiter becomes conjunct with, trines, or forms a sextile with the ruler of the 7th house, this is a good time to look for a boyfriend/girlfriend or spouse. Other aspects will also work, so this is just explaining the basics. Usually aspects show the most strength 3-5 degrees before becoming exact, so you have to get out and try to meet someone just prior to these beneficial aspects reaching their peak. An astrologer can help you with the timing.

Affairs are different than marriage, and are a 5th house matter rather than a 7th house matter. If the 5th house ruler is depressed you are unlikely to have affairs or trysts even if you want one. Men are typically more strongly motivated by sexual urges than women, but sexual activity is a big part of the happiness equation for both men and women and therefore some seek affairs rather than marriage.

Sex is so important to happy relationships that studies show that marriages which increase their sexual activity from once a month to once per week can cause their happiness levels to rise as much as if the couple made an extra $50,000 per year. Married couples tend to have sex about seven times a month, which is about twice a week, while older couples have sex about two to three times per month on average. The number of times you have sex per month corresponds to your age, and that activity lends itself to marital happiness.

A man who is pursuing sexual affairs rather than marriage should want to see Venus, Moon and the Sun in the 5th house whereas a woman should want Mars, Jupiter or the Sun in the 5th. You can actually move or travel to new locations on earth to make this more likely, just as you can move to locations where marriage will become more probable. Pluto in the 5th, which represents sex, is too strong an influence for the house because it usually produces a tendency towards prostitution or the darker sides of sex such as women/men obsessing over the other, sadism, and sexually transmitted diseases. So be careful about fifth house indications if you want to get married or move to a location where affairs will become likely. You want to move to locations where the marriage becomes stronger and better, not threatened. You don't want to move to a location where your partner is likely to have an extramarital affair.

LOCATION

For purposes of romance, master locational astrologer Julian Lee has taught that men might want to permanently move to a location where Venus becomes the ruler of their 7th house, and then (other considerations aside) it becomes more likely that they will marry a beautiful wife. You can also move to put Venus inside the 7th house, and the closer to the cusp the better. If this is not possible, having the Moon rule the seventh house is the next best option for men looking to marry a beautiful woman. In other words, men should move to a location where the Moon or Venus rules their seventh house, but of course this doesn't guarantee marriage, especially if long-term progressions to the 7th house ruler are weak. This little lesson is really over simplistic but gives you an idea of what astrology can tell you.

If women seek a marriage partner, they might consider moving to a location where the seventh house is ruled by Jupiter, Mars or the Sun and where that planet is due to experience extremely strong positive aspects for the next few years, such as secondary progressions, making the likelihood of meeting someone more likely. An astrologer can tell you which planet is best for you because each of the planets will mean something different for your life. Naturally when you move to a new location in order to capture the better astrological influences of that locational chart it will take time for those influences to kick in. Boons will manifest strongest under beneficial planetary transits and progressions, as explained, but of course this will also require your active efforts.

It takes time – up to a year – for a new natal chart to kick in and become the general pattern or template for a new living location. Also, where one house improves because of moving others become worse, hence it is impossible to improve one house and then have all other areas of life improve too. Astrological houses control your money, career, health, fun, spiritual life and so on and moving means you inherit a different set of problems because some houses get better and others get worse. You have to choose what you care most about to make a good move. This is why you must consult an experienced astrologer to interpret these matters. I have simply given you some minor explanations to help get you started.

The best you can do by moving is get a new life where there is more coherency in some particular life areas for particular periods of time. However, you will also lose coherency in other areas of your life too.

HUSBANDS AND WIVES WERE CONNECTED IN THE PAST

You will always be losing something as well as gaining something when you move east or west in a major way to obtain a new natal chart, and those ups and downs will be modified by the strength of positive and negative progressions and transits.

There is no location that is fortunate in all ways and "lucky" for you forever. Any "good fortune" you receive in certain life areas only lasts for a limited time, which can be short or last for years. However, you can indeed stand under an apple tree to catch some falling apples of good fortune if you are smart enough to follow the harvest. But beneficial harvests, where situations are improving or prosperous, only last so long too. As transits and progressions move, any place lucky for love and romance will have its ups and downs, so expect variability in all areas of your life. Nevertheless, you can move to new locations to get the kind of experience harvest that you want.

In India marriages are usually arranged by the parents, so eligible men and woman pray to Heaven to help them find the perfect spouse so that they do not get fixed up with a dud. Because the marriages are usually arranged, those seeking spouses typically recite Vashikaran mantras that beseech help from higher powers to help them find a good husband or wife. Vashikaran mantras exist not just for love, romance and marriage but for other motives as well such as for purely physical relationships.

Mantras are not magic, nor are they evil or

nefarious, nor are they guaranteed to work. They just attract the attention of beings with higher spiritual bodies who can know the thoughts of humans and their past karma, and thus can often give you thoughts that prompt you to meet someone of like mind. Reciting the mantra sufficiently (quite a few times per day over a long period of time) attracts their attention and prompts them to look, but rarely can help be rendered instantly. This is why mantras have to be recited for quite a bit of time before bearing fruit, if at all. If you are seeking a spouse then enlightened beings will know your pain and will try to help, and will help to search for possible partners with compatibility from past karma or because of similar wishes.

Some of these mantras, which are primarily used in India, are as follows:

For a love marriage: Om Hreem Laxmi Narayanaya Namah.

For marriage: Om Kanak Kaa-Kani Aataa Vaataa Shool Raj Panchal Vaancahl Om Yam Yam Yam.

Mantra for marriage: Dam Lam Pam Lam.

Siyar Singhi mantra for getting married: Aim Dam Pam Lam.

Mantra for marriage: Tatou Yayau Rampurogamaiah Shanaiah, Srugal Madhyadiv Bhaghrudhtiah.

Mantra for fast marriage: Om Kleem Mam Karya Siddhi Kari Kari Janaranjini Swaha.

For love: Om Namo Namo Kadsnvari Sarvalok

Vashkari Swaha.

Ganesh mantra for getting married: Om Sri Ganesham Vidhnesham Vivahaharhe Te Namah.

Ganesh mantra for early marriage: Salankrut Kanya Me Dehi Namastyai Ganeshaya Namah.

Mohini mantra to attract your dream partner: Om Namo Mohini Mahamohini Amrut Vaasni Aim Namo Siddha; Guru Ke Paaya Jaanum; Arjun Ke Vaan; Dhaneshwari Ki Mati Bandho; Ghaaun Bando; Paati Meri, Bhakti Guru Ki, Furo Mantra Ishwaro Vaacha.

Mohini mantra for love: Om Namo Anaruthani Ashav Sthani Maharaj Kshani Fatt Soha.

Mantra to remove delay in marriage: Om Hreem Shreem Dram Dreem Kleem Klum Jam Jam Vanakhye Kameshwari Vaadevte Swaha.

Mantra for quick marriage: Om Yagno Pavitram Sahajam Rahat Prajapati Swaha.

Chamunda Devi mantra for marriage: Kleem Aim Hreem Chamundayai Vicche.

Bhairav mantra to remove obstacles in getting married: Om Kaal Bhairavaya Namah.

Special mantra for a happy married life: Om Hum Jum Sah Arhdana-Arishvararupe Hreem Swaha.

Mantra for better husband-wife relations to enhance their love and affection: Om Kshaam Kshem Hreem Hoom Kroum Kraim Fatt.

Kamdev mantra for better husband-wife relations: Mada Mada Mada Maadya Chhile Hreem Amuk

Naagnim Amukswaroopaam Swaha.

Mantra to remove husband-wife differences and produce better domestic harmony: Om Ham Sham Shaam Om Hreem Fatt Swaha.

Mantra to improve sexual relations (act of lovemaking) to be recited during sexual congress: Om Namo Bhagavate Rudraaya Kaamaa Sharaayaa, Striyaa Bhagadraavaya Fatt Fatt Swaha.

Mantra for sexual cultivation as a spiritual practice: Ohm Ah Hung Lah Rah Tah Soh

Shiva mantra for girl's marriage: Om Someshwaraaya Namah.

Katyayani Devi mantra to get a girl married: Om Katyayani Mahamaye.

For a husband: Om Hreem Shreem Kreem Thireem That That Amukam Vasham Karoni.

Mantra to attract a husband: Om Hreem Dhreem Kreem Dhreem Shreem Th Th.

Kartikeya mantra for a girl's marriage: Hreem Kumaraya Namah.

Laxshmi mantra to get a rich husband: Om Shreem Varpradaya Shreem Namah.

Kali Maa mantra for a girl who finds it difficult to get married: Om Aim Hreem Kleem Chamundayai Vicche Namah.

Mantra for getting a good husband per your innermost desires: Hey Gauri Shankara-Dhargini, Yatha Tvam Shankarpriya, Tatha Maa Kuru Kalyani Kaantkantaa Sudurlbhaa.

HUSBANDS AND WIVES WERE CONNECTED IN THE PAST

Mantra for an attractive husband: Tryambakam Jayamahe Sugandhim Pusti-Vardhanam; Urvarukam-Iva Bandhanan Mrtyormuksiya Mamrtat.

Katyayani mantra for an early marriage: Om Katyayani Mahamaye Mahayoginyadheeshwari, Nandgopsutam Devi Patim Me Kurute Namah.

Durga mantra to attract a groom for marriage: Om Gyaninamapi Chetansi Devi Bhagwati Hisa, Baladakrishya Mohay Mahamaya Prayachhati.

Shri Ram mantra to find husband of your dreams: Sunu Siya Satya Asseesa Hamari, Puji Hi Mana Kaamana Tuhari, Narad Vachan Sada Suchi Saacha, So Baru Milihi Jaahim Manu Raacha.

Mantra that a wife can use to reattract their husband's waning interest in them: Namo Mahayakshini Pati Me Vashyam Kuru Kuru Swaha.

Mantra to appear alluring and appealing to men: Om Hreem Kreem Aim Hreem Parmeshwari Swaha.

Mantra to appear alluring and appealing to men: Om Aam Hreem Krom Ehi Ehi Parmeshwari Swaha.

Mantra to attract men: Om Kaam Malini Thah Thah Swaha.

For a beautiful wife: Om Gurve Namah.

For the girl of your dreams: Om Hreem Namah, Om Hreem Namah, Om Om Om Om Om.

Mantra to attract women: Om Kamini Ranjni Swaha.

Mantra to attract women: Om Kumbhni Swaha.

Mantra to attract women: Om Akarshaya.

Mantra to attract women: Om Bhagati Bhag Bhaag

Daayini Amuki Mam Vashym Kuru Kuru Soha.

Mantra for a man seeking a woman from any of the four types of women (Lotus, Artistic, Conch or Elephant): Om Agachch Padmini Soha, Om Agachch Chatrini Soha, Om Agachch Shankhini Soha, Om Agachch Hastini Soha.

Mantra for attracting Padmini type women (soft, tender, beautiful with beautiful complexion): Om Agachch Padmini Swaha.

Mantra for attracting Chatrini type women (artistic temperament): Om Agachch Chatrini Soha

Mantra for attracting Shankhini type women (fiery temperament, passionate and domineering): Om Agachch Shankhini Soha.

Mantra for attracting Hastini type women (coarse, rough woman easy to please who likes sexual pleasure): Om Agachch Hastini Soha.

Mantra to become more beautiful or handsome: Kleem Kamdevaya Namah.

Incidentally, there are even mantras to help with avoiding children or conceiving a baby. Of course, one should depend on science rather than mantras to protect you or help you:

Mantra for birth control: Om Garbhadhaarini, Garbha Stambhanam Kuru Kuru Soha.

Gomti Chakra Mantra to get children: Hili Hili Mili Mili Chili Chili Huk.

HUSBANDS AND WIVES WERE CONNECTED IN THE PAST

Mantra for childless men to gain progeny: Om Hreem Suryaya Namah.

Mantra to help produce a second child: Om Namo Shaktirupaaya Mam Gruhe Putram Kuru Kuru Swaha.

Mantra to ensure smooth pregnancy: Om Shravno Banchgarbhach Sukhmev Prasuyte.

Mantra to help prevent miscarriage: Om Hreem Hreem Chal Chalehu Malehu Th Th Th Swaha.

As stated, if mantras provoke a response this is not magic. Reciting the sounds over and over again every day hundreds of times will cause them to be noticed by enlightened beings (see *Buddha Yoga* and *Nyasa Yoga*) who have taken it upon themselves to help people find what they are looking for, and if you recite them sufficiently it means you really want assistance for your situation. This is why individuals are often instructed to recite mantras for tens of thousands of time in total.

If you recite a mantra that much it shows your sincere desire for help, and gives someone in the spiritual realm sufficient time to see if they can do anything for you. If you recite mantras at times that are astrologically favorable for finding a partner, and do your part in looking too, and if you are in a good location then you will do everything to maximize your chances for a response.

If your motives are negative in any way or the mantra is used for wrong purposes then of course enlightened beings won't help you at all. You're wasting your time if you are asking for help with malefic intentions because this isn't "magic that just works automatically" like some fictitious "attraction secret." Mantras simply ask higher beings to help you, and sometimes they can and sometimes they can't. If you have merit and someone answers the call, they'll certainly see if they can help you. Sometimes they can help and sometimes they won't or cannot. Once again, no one will help you when you have malefic intentions since you will end up hurting other people, and if the timing and circumstances are not right then no one can help you either.

For instance, reciting a mantra for water in a desert won't help you find water, but it might alert some higher spiritual beings to your condition and prompt them to give thoughts to rescue searchers to move in your direction. Karmic causes and conditions are always an impediment to any type of fulfillment you seek. That's why you have to work on making yourself more attractive if you want to attract the opposite sex, and put yourself in the right places at the right times that will maximize your chances. Just as you have to work on a marriage to keep it whole, you have to work at finding a spouse if you want one. Rare and extremely fortunate are those who magically meet the right person right away and just know it.

One of the biggest problems for those seeking mates is being overweight. The truth is that it is a lot easier to maintain your weight than to get fat and try to lose it, and excess weight is a detriment when seeking a spouse. Luckily the cause of weight gain is usually too many grains and sugars in your diet that can easily be avoided. Nevertheless it is just a hard fact that excess weight is a turn-off to prospective partners so here is what you can do.

Diet is more important than going to the gym when you want to get in shape, although if you work on weight training for your arms and legs this will definitely help you improve your appearance. The two simplest ways to lose weight are to subscribe to intermittent fasting and/or a special diet with a little bit of relevant exercise thrown in.

While there are many intermittent fasting schedules, the one that seems easiest and most convenient for losing weight is the 16/8 eating schedule where you eat all of your daily calories within a shortened period, typically 8 hours, and then fast for the remaining 16 hours. To get started you simply pick an eight-hour window and limit your food intake to that time span, such as from 12:00 in the afternoon to 8:00 in the evening. Obviously this means that you would skip breakfast. Other people eat between 9:00 and 5:00 p.m., which allows plenty of time for breakfast around 9 a.m., a normal lunch around 12:00 noon and a light early dinner around 4 p.m. before starting your fast.

One other thing most dieticians or nutritionists don't tell you is that if you want to lose weight then your breakfast should be primarily protein (such as eggs) without any carbohydrates such as toast, bagels, bread, milk or orange juice. Also, in order to lose weight or maintain your weight it is best to eat breakfast within 30 minutes of waking up.

A second way to lose weight quickly is the popular "Slow Carb Diet" promoted by Tim Ferriss in *The 4-Hour Body*:

1. Avoid "white" carbohydrates such as wheat, potatos, bread or multi-grains. No wheat in any form such as bread or pasta either. No white foods means no sugar, rice, potatoes, cheese or cereals. You are essentially trying to avoid sugar and wheat in its many forms, as well as high-glycemic carbohydrates such as rice and potatoes. Just this single rule alone will help many people lose weight.

2. Don't eat fruits because their sugar content will cause you to gain weight when you are trying to lose weight. Avocadoes and tomatoes, which are technically fruits, are permitted.

3. Don't drink calories. In other words, don't drink anything that contains sugar. Coffee, unsweetened tea, water and other beverages without sugar are all allowed. No fruit juices, energy drinks, beer or milk since they contain sugar. Two glasses of red wine per day are

permitted, but no white wine.

4. Eat the same few meals over and over again. There are countless foods available but there are only a handful that will not cause you to gain weight. Once your body gets used to these foods/meals, it tends to metabolize them more quickly so stick with those.

5. Take one day off per week where you can eat anything you want, no questions asked, including bread or fruit and other forms of sugar you would normally avoid. This is a "metabolic spike" day to reset your metabolism to an artificially high rate every week so that your body doesn't think you are in starvation mode, which would slow down weight loss.

Another diet I personally espouse is even simpler. Once again, avoid sugar in any form and "white" carbohydrates (sugar, wheat, rice, potatoes) or grains. For instance, the reason that wheat products are avoided is because they are composed of miniscule flour particles that are too speedily digested. Once in stomach acid, a wheat flour product decomposes into its constituent particles that are transformed into sugar, spike your glucose blood levels, and excess glucose is always turned into fat. So wheat flour products and other high glycemic carbohydrates typically make you gain weight!

Completing the other rules of this diet, don't drink sugar calories like fruit juice and sodas either. You basically avoid sugar, grains and high glycemic foods that turn into sugar quickly. However, you can have up to one piece of fruit per day, but no more. You can also take one day off per week in order to reset your metabolism so that your body doesn't hold onto weight because it thinks you are starving.

Exercise has two options, passive or active, and only needs to be minimal. You can actively exercise using weight training, kettlebells, mini-trampolines, running, biking or swimming. Yoga and Pilates are also options but you should work on toning your arms and thighs with weight training. This is what I prefer for women because a low grain, low sugar diet will take care of their tummies while men will notice they have more toned/muscular arms and thighs due to just a little bit of yoga, Pilates or strength training practice. The weight loss results people usually seek are primarily due to the diet. It's all about the diet!

These diets will help you lose weight in a very short time and will make you much more attractive for the dating game. Or, for the marriage relationship! How? Losing weight can help to rekindle or reignite the sexual flame between spouses that usually declines in all romantic relationships over time. **For your information, therapist and sociology professor Terri Orbuch, who has studied couples for three decades, says that there are three ways to rekindle the sexual** spark in lagging relationships.

Adding an element of mystery and surprise to the relationship (yes, this includes sexy lingerie and roleplaying where weight-loss has played its share) is one such strategy. Another is to engage in fresh, new, novel activities *together* as partners since this creates feelings of excitement that will be transferred onto your spouse. The last strategy is to become involved in arousal-producing activities together such as watching comedies, going to concerts or dances, running races and other activities where you both "feel alive." You might make a habit of showering or bathing together once a week not just to preserve intimacy but to keep communication alive too.

Let's summarize where we've come from. The idea of looking for a relationship leads to the questions of where, when and how, and the strategy of making yourself more attractive. This is turn led to a short discussion on weight loss, which leads to the well-known concept that improving your appearance can even help rekindle the sexual flames between spouses. *Look Younger Live Longer* can also help along these lines as will *Detox Your Body Quickly and Completely*. The common denominator in all these strategies is that they take work. The "in-love" feelings of marriage usually last less than two years so remember that it requires work to find a spouse and requires positive efforts to keep the relationship alive.

CHAPTER 4
PREDICTING AND PREVENTING DIVORCE

Despite the best efforts of couples, today's society tends to pull the marriage partners apart rather than push them together and help them unite as a partnership. Let's see how.

As the divorce rate has climbed, society has begun to think of divorce as normal and this in itself has weakened the marriage bond. As children are increasingly born out of wedlock, this has weakened the family bond too. When television portrays young couples with an affluence that can only be attained after decades of hard work and patience, it instills a dissatisfaction in couples that also can only harm marriages. When both parties in a marriage want to work full time, this also weakens the family bond. When the press teaches both parties that they can "have it all," this unrealistic view harms marriages too.

What most people don't realize is that there are also forces intent on destroying the American family, which are engineered by elites who want to create a different type of society than that dominated by the ideal of strong Christian marriages or marriages at all.

Famous filmmaker Aaron Russo was once interviewed by Alex Jones during which he provided some insight into this matter by recounting a number of conversations he had had with Nick Rockefeller. The famous Rockefeller family is said to be worth billions of dollars and exert an incredibly large influence over policies in America. In a conversation with Aaron Russo, whom Rockefeller often tried to recruit into the Council of Foreign Relations, Nick Rockefeller revealed that the creation of the women's lib movement in America was actually designed to weaken families. Their conversation, as reported to Jones, went as follows:

"Aaron, what do you think women's liberation was all about?"

I said, I had pretty conventional thinking about it at that point ... and I said, "Things about women having the right to work, and getting equal pay as men just as they won the right to vote."

He started to laugh and said, "You're an idiot."

I said, "Why am I an idiot?"

"Let me tell you what that was all about. We the Rockefellers funded that. We funded Women's lib. We're the ones who got it all over the newspapers and television - The

Rockefeller Foundation. And you want to know why? There were two primary reasons. And they were ... One reason was, we couldn't tax half the population before women's lib. And the second reason was, now we get the kids in school at an early age. We can indoctrinate the kids how to think. It breaks up their family. The kids start looking at the state as their family, ... as the school, as the officials as the family not as the parents teaching them."

And so those are the two primary reasons for women's lib, which I thought up to that point was a noble thing. When I saw their intentions behind it, where they were coming from when they created it - the thought of (behind) it - I saw the evil behind what I thought was a noble venture.[5]

Normally, people cannot believe such stories that individuals in power promoted a grand strategy to have public schools eventually substitute for parents, but that is because they are naïve and uninformed. Many people cannot believe that there is such a thing as master plans to socially engineer a nation for specific ends, but most every nation does this and most people simply don't know it.

---

[5] "Reflections and Warnings – An Interview With Aaron Russo," accessed on Mach 1, 2019, https://www.youtube.com/watch?v=YGAaPjqdbgQ.

For this one issue alone, the proof that woman's lib was supported by upper elites was the fact that Gloria Steinem herself admitted that the CIA funded *Ms. Magazine*, which was one of the guiding vehicles for woman's liberation in America. The Central Intelligence Agency does not hand out money to social movements unless it is part of a master plan. It funds people and movements in line with a plan. Its goals were to eventually tax women and break up the nuclear family.

As Nick Rockefeller mentioned, one of the purposes of the women's liberation movement was to slowly transfer family loyalty to more trust in the government, so the design was socialistic. It involved an attitude training agenda where gradually more children would be cared for by the state and indoctrinated to accept certain ideas it wanted to promote. The goal was to affect generations of children this way.

Where previously women used to stay at home to take care of the kids until they reached school age, this parental tradition has now been largely destroyed. Most pre-school children are now deprived of the obvious benefits of growing up in an intact family with the mother at home in their early years. A very large proportion of children is now consigned to daycare, and the traditional family is subsequently shrinking. To compound matters 90% of children today are compelled to attend government schools for twelve to thirteen years where they are exposed to mediocre education, drugs, crime, violence, promiscuity and quite a bit of social programming and political propaganda. Has the family bond strengthened or weakened through this process?

Just as Nick Rockefeller mentioned, the goal of taxing half of the population was also achieved by putting women in the workforce and emptying the home. Feminism advocated the idea of women getting out of the home into the labor market where most of their wages were seized by taxes. Women's liberation thus ended up converting women from "baby factories" to full-time "tax livestock" where their take-home pay was barely more than the family's tax bill. Women won the right to work but they lost the right to raise their family staying at home because it soon required two salaries to support a family and pay all the taxes. In other words, wives were forced out of the motherhood role into an earner's role because high taxation brought an end to single earner families.

Charlotte Thompson Iserbyt, in her research to write *The Deliberate Dumbing of America,* also came across supporting documents for a plan to switch children's allegiances from the family to the state. She held interviews with the managers of philanthropic foundations who stated flat out that the educational decay that we afflict upon children is not just a natural consequence of stupid policies and bad ideas, but is deliberate with a specific agenda. It is funded and guided by unseen hands at upper levels.

HUSBANDS AND WIVES WERE CONNECTED IN THE PAST

Iserbyt used to work in the U.S. Department of Education where she was privy to past and future plans to restructure the American education system. She has come to the conclusion, from reading first-hand documents, that changes gradually brought into the American public education system were done to eliminate the influences of a child's parents, and mold the child in preparation for a socialist-collectivist world of the future. She believes that these changes in our educational system originated from plans formulated primarily by the Rockefeller General Education Board and Andrew Carnegie Foundation for the Advancement of Education. In her writings and interviews she details the psychological methods used to implement and effect the changes. The grand scheme is to produce a dumbed-down society whose working class will serve as labor for a ruling elite.

Why all this fuss? In order to alert you to some of these forces impacting your life so that you can go against them to maintain your marriage and family! First you have to recognize that such programs exist, and then because of your awareness you can fight against these influences in your own life. Most people know nothing about these forces because they just want a happy family life without much interference from the government, and the ability to pay their bills at the end of the month. They just want to be able to run their lives in their own way without any interference from the state, and get justice and protection when they need it.

Marriage, children and families are the fundamental social fabric and bedrock of a nation. If you understand that there are forces working against them then you can then put special effort into your family life to prevent these corrosive forces from negatively affecting you. Don't succumb to the corruption foisted upon you for somebody else's larger social agenda. Couples have enough problems in today's world dealing with marriage difficulties. If they are not aware of these other forces of decay pushing them apart, how can they fight against them?

Buddhist sutras state, "When two people develop intense memories for one another, then in life after life they will be together like an object and its shadow, and they will never be separated." But that doesn't mean that societal influences, imposed from without by the government and powers of the media, won't make it difficult to come together and stay together. The wrong agenda promoted by the government can create a harmful environment for marriage (and family) relationships.

Aaron Russo explained that he only found out this information because he had become influential as a filmmaker and was then wooed by the elites who wanted him to join them. In his famous interview with Alex Jones, which I encourage you to watch on Youtube, he recounted how Nick Rockefeller had told him that the ultimate plan for America was that people should become electronically tagged with chips that would contain their ID and financial information so that they could be controlled. The end goal (agenda) was to get everyone chipped in order to control the whole of society. After chipping, if you said or did something the government didn't like then it would control you by simply turning off your chip and making your money unavailable to you. A chip would make you into a slave of the government where you could be controlled forever.

Once informed, Russo was appalled by the sinister, horrific nature of the plan. He realized that once chipped you effectively became a slave. Also, because of permanent ID tracking you could then be pledged as collateral in perpetual bondage since you couldn't ever escape the system.

When Russo objected to treating the common people as serfs and slaves, Rockefeller had essentially responded, "Why do you care about the common people? What difference do they make to you? What do they mean to you? They're just serfs. Join us and become one of the elite who can ignore them with impunity and whose embedded chip will be coded with special permissions and allowances. You should take care of yourself first."

Some people have a hard time believing such stories but along these lines a Soviet KGB defector, Yuri Bezmenov, was once interviewed by historian G. Edward Griffin where he also explained how the Soviets used long-term master plans to destabilize foreign nations that didn't even know they were under attack. Bezmenov said that it typically takes around twenty years to educate (program) a generation of students so that they become unable to assess facts correctly. His testimony confirmed that countries create social engineering agendas to accomplish missions, in this case long-term plans to destabilize other nations, just as the CIA and Rockefeller planned to do through women's liberation and the plans that were to follow in its wake. Russo thought women's lib was a great thing, but was aghast when he found out it was part of a greater plan whose real mission was to destabilize and weaken the American family and society. So even America does this too.

Bezmenov's interview is fascinating if only to awaken people to the forces that are really attacking the American family, and which people must fight against to keep marriages and families strong and vital. It is my firm belief that there is also a carefully orchestrated agenda in the United States to weaken the Christian values that built the nation and define the majority of its people, which will then weaken the country's moral fiber and leave America open to decadence and decline.

When Boris Bajanov, Stalin's personal secretary, defected to the West in 1928 he also disclosed that the Kremlin's primary foreign policy was to use covert means to weaken foreign countries from within by sowing propaganda, disinformation and hoodwinking foreign intellectuals to act against their own interests. Ultimately the Soviets would try to control the narrative taking hold within a foreign nation and try to lead it down errant paths in this way. The destruction of the American family and family values falls right into this type of campaign, which was called "reflexive control" by the Soviets.

Bezmenov's message to America, which was more detailed than Bajanov's warning, is extremely instructive for he revealed that the Soviets, in order to destabilize a country, would actively recruit intellectuals, leftists and other high stage players who could be bought. These are the people whose activities end up swaying public opinion and who end up persuading the public to adopt their ideals that never work out according to their pet theories. While they call themselves progressives they are usually just radical leftists.

Socialism and Communism are but two examples of movements initiated and fostered by intellectuals that have had a great destructive force on the world. Sold as future utopias to the public that never ever manifest, they actually work against the strength of the family and destroy the fiber of nations. A portion of the interview ("Deception Was My Job") between Bezmenov and Griffin on such topics went as follows:

> Griffin: Our conversation is with Yuri Alexander Bezmenov. Mr. Bezmenov was born in 1939 in a suburb of Moscow. He was

the son of a high ranking Soviet officer. He was educated in the elite schools inside the Soviet Union and he became an expert in Indian culture and Indian languages. He had an outstanding career with Novesti, which was the, and still is I should say, the press arm or the press agency of the Soviet Union. It turns out that this is also a front for the KGB. He escaped to the West in 1970 after becoming totally disgusted with the Soviet system, and he did this at great risk to his life. He certainly is one of the world's outstanding experts on the subject of Soviet propaganda and disinformation and active measures.

Mr. Bezmenov, the Soviets use the phrase "Ideological Subversion." What do they mean by that?

Bezmenov: Ideological subversion is the process which is legitimate overt and open, you can see it with your own eyes. All you can do, all Americans needs to do is to unplug their bananas from their ears, open up their eyes and they can see. There is no mystery. It has nothing to do with espionage. I know that espionage and intelligence gathering looks more romantic, it sells more to the audience through the advertising, probably. That's why your Hollywood producers are so crazy about

James Bond type of thrillers. But in reality, the main emphasis of the KGB is not in the area of intelligence at all. According to my opinion and the opinion of many defectors of my caliber, only about fifteen percent of time, money and manpower is spent on espionage as such. The other eighty-five percent is a slow process which we call either ideological subversion or active measures, or psychological warfare. What it basically means is, to change the perception of reality, of every American, to such an extent that despite an abundance of information no one is able to come to sensible conclusions in the interest of defending themselves, their family, their community and their country.

It's a great brainwashing process, which goes very slow and is divided into four basic stages. The first one being demoralization. It takes from fifteen to twenty years to demoralize a nation. Why that many years? Because this is the minimum number of years required to educate on generation of students in the country of your enemy, exposed to the ideology of the enemy. In other words, Marxism, Leninism ideology is being pumped into the soft heads of at least three generations of American students, without being challenged or contra-balanced by the basic values of Americanism, American patriotism.

Most of the activity of the department was to compile huge amount, volume of information on individuals who were instrumental in creating public opinion. Publishers, editors, journalists, actors, educationalists, professors of political science, members of Parliament, representatives of business circles. Most of these people were divided roughly in two groups. Those who were told the Soviet foreign policy, they would be promoted to the positions of power through media and public opinion manipulation. Those who refuse the Soviet influence in their country would be character assassinated, or executed physically contra-revolution. Same was as in a small town named HEWA in South Vietnam. Several thousand so of Vietnamese were executed in one night when the city was captured by Vietcong for only two days. And American CIA could never figure out, how could possibly Communists know each individual, where he lives, where to get him, and would be arrested in one night, basically in some four hours before dawn, put on a van, taken out of the city limits and shot. The answer is very simple, long before communists occupied the city there was an extensive network of informers, local Vietnamese citizens who knew absolutely everything about people who are instrumental in public opinion including barbers and taxi drivers. Everybody who was sympathetic to the United States was executed. Same thing was done under the guidance of the Soviet Embassy in Hanoi, and same thing I was doing in New Delhi. To my horror I discovered that in the files where people were doomed to execution there were names of pro-soviet journalists with whom I was personally friendly.

Griffin: Personally?

Bezmenov: Yes! They were idealistically-minded leftists who made several visits to USSR and yet the KGB decided that contra-revolution or drastic changes in the political structure of India, they would have to go.

Griffin: Why's that?

Bezmenov: Because [laughs] they know too much. Simply, because you see, the useful idiots, the leftists who are idealistically believing in the beauty of [the] Soviet socialist or Communist or whatever system, when they get disillusioned, they become the worst enemies. That's why my KGB instructors specifically made the point: never bother with leftists. Forget about these political prostitutes. Aim higher.

This was my instruction: try to get into large-circulation, established conservative media; reach filthy-rich movie makers; intellectuals, so-called 'academic' circles; cynical, egocentric people who can look into your eyes with angelic expression and tell you a lie. These are the most recruitable people: people who lack moral principles, who are either too greedy or too [much] suffer from self importance. They feel that they matter a lot. These are the people who[m] [the] KGB wanted very much to recruit.

Griffin: But to eliminate the others, to execute the others? Don't they serve some purpose; wouldn't they be the ones you rely on?

Bezmenov: No. They serve [a] purpose only at the stage of destabilization of a nation. For example, your leftists in [the] United States: all these professors and all these beautiful civil rights defenders. They are instrumental in the process of the subversion only to destabilize a nation. When their job is completed, they are not needed any more. They know too much.

Some of them, when they get disillusioned, when they see that Marxist-Leninists come to power—obviously they get offended—they think that they will come to power. That will never happen, of course. They will be lined up against the wall and shot.

But they may turn into the most bitter enemies of Marxist-Leninists when they come to power. And that's what happened in Nicaragua. You remember most of these former Marxist-Leninists were either put [in] prison, or one of them split and now he is working against [the] Sandinistas. It happened in Grenada, when Maurice Bishop was—he was already a Marxist—he was executed by a new Marxist, who was more Marxist than this Marxist.

[The] same happened in Afghanistan, when first there was [Nur Mohammad] Taraki, he was killed by [Hafizullah] Amin, [and] then Amin was killed by Babrak Karmal with the help of [the] KGB. [The] same happened in Bangladesh when [Sheikh] Mujibur Rahman, [a] very pro-Soviet leftist, was assassinated by his own Marxist-Leninist military comrades. It's the same pattern everywhere. The moment they serve their purpose, all these useful idiots [will] either be executed entirely (or the idealistically-minded Marxist) or exiled, or put in prisons like in Cuba. Many former Marxists are in Cuba—I mean in prison.

So most of the Indians who were cooperating with the Soviets, especially with our Department of Information of the USSR embassy, were listed for execution. And when I discovered that fact, of course I was sick: I was mentally and physically sick. I thought that I [was] going to explode one day during the briefing of the Ambassador's office; I would stand up and say something [like,] "We are basically a bunch of murderers. That's what we are. It has nothing to do with 'friendship and understanding between the nation[s]' and blah-blah-blah. We are murderers! We behave as [a] bunch of thugs in a country which is hospitable to us, a country with ancient traditions."[6]

The point of recounting this interview is to make you realize that when the KGB wants to influence or destabilize a nation it uses useful idiots who tend to be leftist intellectuals spouting blue-sky notions that cannot match with the realities of human behavior. In today's America, unfortunately you find a large

---

[6] "Yuri Bezmenov: Deception Was My Job," accessed on March 1, 2019, https://www.youtube.com/watch?v=YGAaPjqdbgQ.

proportion of such leftists and "strange notion" liberals in the Democratic party as well as the Communist party. And on TV!

When a certain strata of the powerful elite in American want to move it in a certain direction, they too develop a long-term plan that they begin to execute. As part of this plan they also look for useful idiots with influence who can publicly promote some fantasy of virtue that conflicts with the realities of human nature such as male-female relationships. Many of their unrealistic utopian ideas actually erode values-centered modes of thinking, which is the opposite of what we want in a healthy society. Their policies are designed to destabilize culture and soften the moral fiber of the nation that keep marriages and families strong and healthy.

In our case, if you look around you then you will see that marriage and family bonds have steadily weakened over the last few decades because of various societal forces and themes promoted through the media. For instance, society no longer pushes couples to try to work things out and stay together. If you really want to maintain a strong marriage and family then you must adopt stronger family values and make efforts to work against negative influences. Marriages take work that includes commitment to a partner through thick and thin. Couples especially need to learn the skills needed to communicate better, resolve conflicts peacefully, and bring about a harmonious unity. One cannot expect instant togetherness just as you cannot expect instant prosperity, but these unrealistic expectations seem to be the message promoted through TV.

In any case, the divorce rate is now approximately 50-60% in American society, and people are more likely to divorce than to stay together. When we include couples that do not marry but cohabitate and then split up, we can say that the divorce rate is even higher.

Where in earlier days both partners gave up their ego to the marriage bond, accepting that each had a certain role/responsibility to play within the marriage and each should equally try to add to their partner's life, now each party often immediately thinks about themselves first and considers that a compromise or sacrifice means they are losing to the other party. After a sacrifice, in today's world the marriage partners feel "compromised" and unsatisfied. Is this strengthening marriages?

Of course some conflicts cannot be resolved with compromises but must be managed. No one should expect that you can solve all marriage issues, so some will simply remain and must be managed over time. When you marry another person you automatically pick someone who represents some unresolvable conflicts (perpetual issues) for the rest of your life. We all have sets of these issues, even irritating qualities, due to personality differences. If you marry someone else you simply inherit a different set of unresolvable conflicts because each person comes with their own set of flaws. This is why you need to avoid the deal breaker individuals at the start. You must eliminate the incompatible partners even if you have karma with them.

Couples will rarely see eye to eye on every issue or solve every conflict, so marriage conflicts aren't about being right as much as about kindly finding resolutions that both partners can live with. For those situations where both couples continue to disagree, you simply have to manage the conflict. However, when marital disagreements turn to constant criticism, anger or fighting then marriage becomes a negative competitive game where couples forget to see each other as a friend, but instead think of the other as an adversary. If the marriage becomes too toxic in this way then divorce is probably the outcome.

In the best of worlds, marriages are a team where the partners make sacrifices for and to the union – to the marriage bond – not for the other party. Couples should realize this before they get married, which is why I said that there has to be a guiding vision or joint goal of the marriage. If the person you are dating cannot fulfill that envisioned role of equal effort from both parties then you shouldn't marry them or even date them for a long time unless there are benefits you both agree on getting from that state of affairs. The point is that for a marriage to work you must sacrifice your ego to the rope of the marriage bond rather than to the other party.

A marriage shouldn't be a power struggle where

each party tries to win points or change the other into how they think the other should be like. It should be a unified team with shared interests and ideals where the couple wants to move in a certain direction to build something together.

"Me versus you" conflicts and confrontations can be turned into a "we'll get through this together" collaboration if couples are taught how to do this. It is not that arguments should not arise because they always will. How couples deal with disagreements is the important thing. Marriages aren't "bad" just because there are a few unresolvable issues that require management rather than resolution. When most marriages have a few unresolvable issues where the partners simply learn to accept each other's choices, the disagreements rarely lead to divorce.

Can you predict the likelihood of divorce? If we don't use some fantastic method such as *Tieh Pan Shen Shu* or the *nadi granthas*, then we must turn to science and the statistics of divorce. There are many statistics that predict when couples will have a higher chance of divorcing. This incudes the bride having pre-wedding jitters, the couple marrying too young or after age thirty-two, a shotgun wedding where the duo marry due to an unplanned pregnancy, the fact that divorce runs in the family (making the pattern mentally easier to duplicate), one party smokes but the other does not (a difference in values), the wife makes more money than the husband (so is less dependent upon him for support, or is more like an alpha male herself), one of the partners is too controlling or thinks they are always right (are not influenceable), too much joint debt that will produce financial strain, or the wife is much older than the husband.

Age is important. There is an old rule that you should not be dating someone who is far younger than you, and similarly far older than you. A general rule is that if you take half of your age and then add seven, this is the minimum age that you should ever date.

Another rule developed by mathematicians, which is fun to know but probably impractical, is that women looking for the best husband should date 37% of their expected lifetime pool of available suitors, and then pick the first one who is better than anyone else they have dated previously. This rule mathematically maximizes a woman's chances of finding the best suitor. You can also apply this rule to the time you expect to spend in dating before marriage; you should date various suitors for 37% of that expected time and then pick the first suitor who is better than all the previous others. This will "mathematically" maximize your chances of finding the best mate, but of course this is just an unrealistic bit of fun.

Emory University studied 3,000 American couples to determine factors that predicted divorce. It analyzed all sorts of metrics such as income levels, the attractiveness of partners, wedding attendance and other statistics they could measure. Their findings were that couples who wanted to minimize their chances for divorce should date for three years before getting engaged. Furthermore, being wealthy helps with marriage longevity but potential partners should not be gold-diggers, especially women. When getting married the wedding can be large but should be cheap (not extravagantly expensive), and the couple should never skip their honeymoon.

University of Virginia researcher E. Mavis Hetherington PhD studied 1,400 families over thirty years to come up with his own divorce predictors. He found that certain types of marriages/couples were prone to divorce due to an incompatibility of habits or personalities, such as where one partner might press to solve problems but the other might regularly dismiss the partner's concerns. He also found that low-risk marriages were those where the husband and wife viewed themselves as a team.

The best single source for understanding and preventing divorce is probably John Gottman PhD who has written several books on his research – *The Seven Principles for Making Marriage Work, The Relationship Cure, What Makes Love Last?, Why Marriages Succeed or Fail,* and *Ten Lessons to Transform Your Marriage.* How does Gottman say that you prevent divorce? First we have to identify the biggest, most destructive predictors of separation, and then minimize those factors in your relationship.

Gottman found that there are four negative,

corrosive patterns of marital interaction that escalate conflicts between partners and typically destroy marriages. He called these behavioral patterns "The Four Horsemen of the Apocalypse." They are criticism, defensiveness, contempt and stonewalling. He found that couples which separate all strongly exhibit at least one of these toxic behaviors. From his findings, here are the four toxic behaviors that are marriage killers that must be minimized in a relationship.

CRITICISM

Criticism is finding fault in your partner's character. It involves taking your partner's behavior and then turning it into a negative statement about their character, namely criticizing the type of person they are. It is suggesting that your partner's personality is defective. Using the words, "You always" or "you never" are common criticisms that frame the cause of an argument as being due to a deficiency in the other person. In criticizing your partner, rather than their behavior, you imply that they have negative personality traits. For instance, "You always talk about yourself. You are so selfish."

The general rule in interpersonal relations is that if you want to provide criticism to another you should never criticize the person but *focus on criticizing their behavior*. On the other hand, when you criticize your partner you basically imply that they have a character flaw and there is something wrong with them. Hearing such criticism, your partner is most likely to respond defensively because they feel under attack. Over time, the personal detractions in these interactions can add up, feeding darker feelings of resentment and contempt that can accumulate into a large mass of negative emotions. You cannot let little slights and issues build and build in a marriage until the dam finally breaks because then there is no possibility of repair.

The antidote to criticism is to make a direct complaint about improper behavior, and not your significant other, that is not a global attack on their personality. You must avoid phrases that aren't constructive in conversations like, "You're so selfish." If couples enter into a common pattern of negativity then it will be hard to exit that pattern. When one partner becomes very judgmental of the other this is definitely a sign that a relationship is in jeopardy and you have to take remedial measures immediately.

One master at handling criticism told me they first point a finger at themselves and then gently bring up the situation that must be discussed. Or, as one marriage counselor said, learn to "Keep your mouth shut and don't act out." When asked the secret of a good marriage, Billy Graham's wife aptly said, "The secret of a happy marriage is two good forgivers." If interested, Dr. Gary Chapman teaches five ways for couples to apologize to one another – *The Five Languages of Apology*.

DEFENSIVENESS

When you feel under attack then as a natural reaction you will get defensive to protect yourself. Defensiveness is when you attempt to protest against a perceived injustice such as undue criticism. Typically you go on the counterattack to defend yourself, but some people play the victim instead. For instance, if your partner says you are late, a typical sort of counterattacking response is, "It's not my fault we're always late. It's your fault."

The best way to handle situations that provoke a defensive response is to say, "Talk to me, I want to hear how you feel." Taking responsibility for your role in a tough situation is uncomfortable, but this response keeps a bad situation from escalating and worsening. If you can reduce defensiveness by turning it into a search for understanding you can eliminate one of the best predictors of divorce.

CONTEMPT

Contempt is when you talk down to your partner, expressing resentment often with anger, disgust or insults. When you are insulting or condescending to your partner in a way where you take yourself as superior then this is showing contempt for the other. It is an expression from a relative position of superiority where one party is projecting, "I don't think very highly of you" or "I am better than you." Mocking your partner, calling them names, insulting them, rolling your eyes and sneering in disgust are all examples of contempt where you are putting your partner beneath you.

Contempt destroys your ability to maintain positive views about your partner as well as the idea that you are equal partners. With that deterioration of seeing your partner as beneath you the likelihood of divorce rises.

Of all the four horsemen, contempt is the most serious. Contemptuous put-downs will destroy the fondness and admiration there once was between a couple at their beginnings, and will basically destroy the relationship. It is "the kiss of death" that is the best predictor of divorce. Once contempt takes hold within a relationship, forever after the partners will tend to see each other in a negative way by default. It is very hard to reverse this mindset once it becomes an ingrained habit.

The antidote to contempt within a relationship is to avoid put-downs of each other and actively work on building up a culture of appreciation that requires regular appreciative habits and counters to disrespect. Both of you must create a mental habit of scanning the environment for things you appreciate that the other is doing or has done, and then let them know it. Otherwise, if you let contempt take hold then the negativity will begin to feed on itself and simple normal interactions may spiral into a perpetual zone of negativity.

STONEWALLING

Stonewalling happens when a listener tunes out, shuts down, or emotionally withdraws from a conversation. In stonewalling a listener basically withdraws from interactions with another person. A stonewaller in a conversation (interaction) won't even give a speaker the usual nonverbal clues that they are listening anymore. They'll stop "tracking" the speaker while in their presence, or they might even leave the room as an escape because they don't want to deal with the situation anymore.

In stonewalling an individual basically turns off or shuts down which conveys the message, "I don't want to participate." They send a message to the other party that they don't care enough to fight through the discomfort of the situation, or simply don't want to.

Stonewalling, in all its various forms, is one of the four reactions that strongly predict divorce. It most often applies to men because they have a tendency to cross their arms, abandon eye contact, or look to the side and to stop tracking a conversation if it is unpleasant when difficult things come up.

A stonewaller may look like they don't care but that usually isn't the case. Typically they are overwhelmed and are trying to calm themselves by shutting down, but their partner usually assumes they don't care enough about the problem to talk about it.

In a marriage relationship, we might find a tendency for one person who demands to talk about uncomfortable topics but the other looks for escape, and thus we'll see stonewalling. The antidote is to learn to identify the signs that you or your partner is starting to feel emotionally overwhelmed and to agree together to take a break when a discussion becomes too formidable for anyone to handle. If the problem still needs discussion then you can pick it up when you are both calmer. This is how to defuse the problem of stonewalling and situations too hot to handle.

Gottman also found that there were three behaviors you can practice until they become natural that helped defeat the four horsemen and keep marriages strong. They are principles for building a successful relationship.

The first is responding positively to "bids" within a relationship. All throughout the day marriage partners are constantly making "bids" for each other's attention in order to form a connection. A bid is a quick "ping" looking for an affectionate response from the partner, an instant connection between the spouses. It is an attempt to generate a small moment of positive attention. One partner makes a small move hoping to elicit a positive response from their spouse to show interest in their interest.

When we respond successfully to bids by turning towards them rather than away, and by not turning them into a fight, then we strengthen the relationship. By always turning toward the other we build a *history of connection* that strengthens the relationship.

Responding to bids is a little thing that makes a big difference when done over and over again because successful bids add up into a strong unifying bond. It's like a video game where each response you give receives a point that accumulates into a total higher score, and thus the relationship is further strengthened by regular, continuous tiny acts of attention and consideration.

Lasting love is all about attention to small stuff done over and over again like this. For a marriage to go from good to great you must develop consistent, habitual behaviors that reunify your bond and keep the marriage strong and healthy. Since most marriage difficulties occur due to poor communication issues and losing connection with the spouse you must institutionalize ways to renew your bonding and level of communications like this.

Gottman found that couples who divorced had turned toward bids only 33% of the time whereas couples who stayed married had turned toward bids 86% of the time. If you want your marriage to become stronger then turn toward your partner when they are speaking, and if they want you to notice something *then look at it!* Making strong eye contact with our partner and listening with intent are ways to tell your partner they are important. Don't always ignore your partner because you are busy with something else. This disinterest or neglect, for someone who shares the same bed, can become a dangerous habit that leads to divorce.

Another aspect to the necessity of responding to bids is emotional responsiveness. Sue Johnson, a clinical psychologist in Ottawa, said, "The most important thing we've learned, the thing that totally stands out in all of the developmental psychology, social psychology and our lab's work in the last 35 years is that the secret to loving relationships and to keeping them strong and vibrant over the years, to falling in love again and again, is emotional responsiveness."

Couples are always looking for emotional, communication and other connections with their spouses. Most partners don't feel they have a secure base or safe haven with their significant other without those connections, so you must continuously supply those connection points. Don't become disinterested in your spouse and start to neglect them. Send out pings, and respond to them too. Give hugs and smiles, touch one another, and say kind words to reaffirm your bonding. Make this a regular habit to show your fondness and appreciation for the other with tiny acts. This is the second technique for building a relationship.

Gottman also revealed that a powerful strategy for building a relationship and keeping it alive is to build up a "Love Map" of your spouse. To maintain the friendship and intimacy of the relationship he suggested that couples frequently ask open-ended questions of one another (e.g. "What is it that worries you about X?") to derive a picture of their intimate world. Once you both build up a map of your partner's world to gain a deeper intimate knowledge of them then it becomes easier to shift with the challenges that come to you both over time. You are not the same person at age forty as you were at age twenty, and you will change during the marriage as well. Therefore the "state of the union" has to be continually updated as well as the "fit" or expectations for you two as a couple over time. One bit of advice is to set monthly "state of the union" meetings with your spouse on the health of your marriage, such as two hours per month, so you can keep intimate communications alive with these open-ended questions and update your joint expectations.

Another thing to do to strengthen a marriage is to emphasize the positive perspective and celebrate the hard times you and your spouse have both been through together. All long-term relationships have ups and downs, but too often couples think about all the negative aspects of their relationship when they should be remembering their past triumphs together over adversity. You should frequently reemphasize your good memories with your spouse as well as enthusiastically embrace good news with attention and interest. Always look at how far you have come together rather than how far you yet have to go.

It is very important for couples to celebrate new

triumphs together such as when someone gets a promotion or raise, sells something they created, gets recognized in the press and so forth. Science shows that when couples celebrate their partner's accomplishments as if they were their own, for they are a team, they tend to be more satisfied in the relationship. In a good marriage you are the other person's cheerleader.

Couples who not only celebrate their triumphs but strive to have new experiences together, or who simply share common experiences together on a regular basis (such as walking together, dining at restaurants as a couple, cooking together, listening to music together etcetera) also tend to become more loving and supportive of one another. Adventuring together, and doing things that are novel and fun together, tends to release "feel good" hormones that can help to cement a relationship in a stronger way. And doing ordinary things together that involve common interests harkens back to one of our five relationship compatibilities - that a couple should try to share enjoyable activities with one another.

The last bit of advice for keeping a marriage strong is to frequently say positive things to your partner. There should be far more positive interactions than negative ones with your partner. In fact, studies show that there are a minimum of five times more positive interactions than negative ones in the marriages that are happiest. Again, *there are five times more positive stuff than negative stuff in the communication interactions for the marriages that work!* You might consider this preponderance of good stuff over bad as a way to fulfill the need to constantly renew courtship. On the other hand, couples who divorced tended to have less than one happy encounter for every negative interaction.

What's a "positive interaction"? Giving your partner a compliment, showing your appreciation for something (however big or small), reliving a fun memory, or just affectionately doing something nice for them such as touching them on the shoulder. When you create a history of constantly showing fondness, admiration and appreciation for your spouse in small ways then this will definitely build your relationship. It is quite easy to improve a relationship simply by starting to compliment your partner in some way each and every day, leaving a cute note where your spouse will find it, smiling at your spouse with a long smile, or simply touching them in a loving way. Never underestimate the power of physical affection. A good marriage is created and maintained by consistent, habitual positive behaviors.

The short of it is that you have to work on a marriage to keep it strong. Even a very strong karmic marriage requires work. Even between soulmates various frictions will arise over time, but now you know the major marriage sore spots to avoid that typically produce divorce and how to reduce, eliminate and defuse those frictions.

CHAPTER 5
BEGETTING AND RAISING CHILDREN

Many couples want children, but often cannot conceive. Sometimes couples have the opposite desire of not wanting children at all, or want to wait until the time is right. Many couples are "not sure" about their marriage and its potential longevity so they want to delay having children to protect themselves, especially since children are no less than a multi-decade commitment that might have to be shouldered without the other parent.

Others want some initial free time to spend with their spouse before they engage in the time-consuming task of raising children, or still want to devote some time to their careers, and they especially want to avoid children during the initial two-year honeymoon period of the marriage where they are enjoying the high of romantic love when small disconnects and flaws go unnoticed. They are usually interested in birth control because there are things they still want to do and experience before they assume the commitment of taking care of children.

Sometimes a marriage doesn't seem to be going

anywhere or the couple's careers aren't progressing, and then they get the idea that children might solve their issues. Rarely do children solve marital dissatisfaction. In those cases, having children is just a distraction that keeps a couple busy and occupied with a family rather than committed to one another. After begetting children, the commitment to the spouse usually turns into a commitment to the family that keeps everyone busy, but which doesn't really solve any deeper issues or hold the couple together if they didn't initially view themselves as a team that wanted to build something deeper together.

You must also understand that after couples have children, marriage usually becomes less important to their happiness than the overall family dynamic. After the arrival of children, the focus usually shifts to the family unit. You must think carefully before having children, such as whether you want the commitment and are really qualified to take on the responsibility of being parents in the first place.

Fertility issues are a problem that has plagued mankind for millennia, and there are several things you should know that might help your marriage if the wife wants to get pregnant.

Most women have been taught to know their fertility cycle and when they are most likely to become pregnant according to the cycles of menstruation. With thermometer in hand, off to the bedroom couples rush at the time of the month when the wife is most likely to conceive. However, some women find that they still cannot get pregnant, so here are a few pointers.

Most infertility clinics are *detoxification centers* that afterwards put women on fertility herbs to maximize their chances for pregnancy. If a woman's body has accumulated too many poisons over time, such as frequently happens with hairdressers who have absorbed too many chemicals, her body will not allow conception in order to protect a baby. Once a woman undergoes a detoxification regimen, however, her body recognizes that she has reduced some potential problems and it usually becomes much easier to get pregnant.

I have put many standard detoxification protocols in *Detox Cleanse Your Body Quickly and Completely* that any woman can use to help prepare herself for pregnancy. A woman should undergo a sufficient detoxification cleanse prior to when she wants to get pregnant, and then start taking multi-vitamins and fertility herbs before the time she wants to conceive.

Sperm counts are dropping across the world for a variety of reasons, so for a successful pregnancy it is important for the man to do his part by maximizing his fertility too. Zinc supplements (50-100 mg daily along with copper) will increase sperm counts, and megadoses of vitamin C for a few weeks (6,000 mg per day) will also increase sperm production. Source Naturals Ultimate Ascorbate C is a great brand of vitamin C that I often use. This two-part protocol will produce more sperm, stronger sperm, and better swimming sperm that will, as a natural result, maximize the chances of pregnancy.

With a woman having detoxified (purified) her body, ingesting fertility herbs along with vitamins, and a man taking zinc and vitamin C, you've done a lot to maximize the chances for pregnancy. The woman should also eliminate vegetable oils and sugar from her diet, which often ends infertility by itself. The rest is timing and help from Heaven such as prayers and mantras already provided.

Anything else? Remember, it is also essential that prenatal vitamins start to be taken *several weeks before conception* to prepare for the first few weeks of pregnancy, which is when the most fundamental decisions about the shape and health of a baby's body will be made. This is the time to especially take vitamin supplements to prevent birth defects, especially B-vitamins and minerals.

Therefore if you want to get pregnant and you want your baby to have a perfect body without defects you should start taking multivitamins *well before* the pregnancy, as well as *during* pregnancy too. Freeda Vitamins are a great brand (they make the best B-vitamins in the world) and so are Thorne Research and SuperNutrition Vitamins. Remember to also *eliminate sugar and vegetable oils from the diet.*

As stated, there is the matter of the best timing to try to conceive a baby, which is a topic we will now discuss.

The Billings Method can be used for natural birth control and also to determine the best timing for pregnancy efforts. It is also known as the Ovulation Method or Mucus Method. It was developed by Drs. John and Evelyn Billings of Melbourne, Australia in response to the fact that the Rhythm Method for pregnancy or birth control is not reliable. The birth control failure rate is 1.2% whereas according to John Billings, "The combined biological failure rate and user rate of the ovulation method in Tonga was 0.69 percent." The technique, which you can read about in *The Ovulation Method*, is as follows.

"The Billings Method is a one-step reading of a woman's cervical mucus, performed by the woman herself in a moment and without internal examination. Every day, she gently wipes her labia with clean, dry, white toilet paper. She looks at the paper to see if there is any mucus on it. If there is, she is likely to be fertile. If the mucus is wet and slippery, and can be easily stretched, then she is very fertile. If the paper stays dry, she is likely to be infertile that day. On the day of the most wet, slippery, clear mucus, she is most fertile of all. This day is called the peak day, and is the very day she ovulates. She will also feel wettest on this day. She remains fertile for three days after the peak.

"It does not matter how old the woman is, nor does it matter how long her menstrual cycles are. Unlike the Rhythm Method, there is no need for regular menstrual cycles. There is no need to fit into a normal, clockwork 28-day model. If a woman has short menstrual cycles, she will ovulate early. If they are long, she will ovulate late. The mucus is there at ovulation, regardless. If she misses a period, there will simply have been no ovulation, and therefore no fertile, wet mucus that cycle. A woman does not even have to know to read and write to use the Billings Method effectively. Trials in the South Pacific nation of Tonga between 1970 and 1972 showed high levels of acceptance and success with the Billings Method.

"Abnormal temperature, such as a low fever, will interfere with the temperature method of birth control. It will not obstruct accurate readings with the Billings method, however. Abnormal vaginal discharges, also, do not prevent a woman from recognizing her state of fertility. Given the knowledge, any woman can use the Billings Method for her entire reproductive lifetime without financial cost. And, obviously, unlike medical methods of birth control, there are no harmful side effects with the Billings Method."[7]

Such information can be combined with the findings of Czech psychiatrist Dr. Eugen Jonas, reported within *Astrological Birth Control* (Sheila Ostrander and Lynn Schroeder), if his method indeed

---

[7] Andrew Saul, *Doctor Yourself*, (Basic Health Publications, North Bergen: New Jersey, 2003), pp. 96-97.

works. Dr. Jonas wished to help the many women who desired pregnancy and who had been trying in vain for a long time. Based on studying thousands of pregnancies, he claimed to find that the times of the greatest fertility for women were based on the relationship of the Sun and the Moon at the time of the woman's birth - the same phase of the moon as that in which the woman was born. In other words, if a woman was born with the Sun and Moon at a 60-degree angle, as occurs five days after the New Moon, she would each month become fertile when the Sun and Moon were at a 60-degree angle and for a period on either side of this period.

To avoid pregnancy, Jonas suggests that a couple should abstain from sex on (and for several days prior to) the day that the Sun and Moon repeat the exact angle they made with each other at the moment of the woman's birth. A woman born at the exact moment of the full moon would abstain during, and for several days just prior to, the full moon since that's when she would also be highly fertile. Since sperm can survive for as long as three days it is recommended that one abstain from sex for three days before the repeated phase angle if you want to avoid pregnancy. If you want a baby, this is an additional time to enter into the bedroom.

When combined with abstention during ovulation this modified rhythm method, according to Czech researchers, is 98% effective for birth control.

I have some doubts about this methodology and

feel it is questionable, but also believe you should be told about it because someone may one day research it and find that it does work. At worst it simply indicates some extra days to enter the bedroom and get busy if you want to conceive a baby, or some extra days of restraint. Does it work? I really don't know, but couples might have fun finding out so there is no harm in telling you about it.

Once pregnant, every woman desires a healthy baby and also wants to avoid a miscarriage. Famous progesterone specialist Dr. John Lee taught that natural progesterone cream would help prevent miscarriages, especially for women who had had repeated miscarriages. It was especially helpful to women who were getting older and worried about pregnancy due to their age. Various cultures also recommend different foods for preventing a miscarriage as well.

Are there any other useful natural remedies that might benefit you for common pregnancy conditions?

Ginger is used in the East to prevent the nausea of pregnancy, although a study shows that nausea can usually be stopped entirely within three days by taking 5 mg of vitamin K3 together with 25 mg of vitamin C.

Thomas Brewer MD reduced pre-eclampsia and eclampsia conditions of pregnancy in nearly every hospital and clinic where he was in charge with one simple measure – a high protein diet. When a woman develops eclampsia during pregnancy then a high protein diet can end it.

The main secrets to having a healthy baby are eating an extremely healthy diet, avoiding poisons, living a peaceful life without too much stress, and taking multi-vitamin supplements. Most everyone knows that pregnant women should avoid alcohol, drugs and cigarettes, but what they don't know is that taking large doses of vitamin C helps hold a pregnancy from the start and is essential for helping a child form strong connective tissue that it will have for the rest of its life. B-vitamins help prevent birth defects too.

Dr. Frederick Klenner MD gave very large doses of vitamin C to over 300 pregnant women and found no complications in any of the pregnancies or deliveries, but did notice that the "vitamin C babies" were the healthiest and happiest of all the babies delivered. Specifically, Klenner gave 4,000 mg during the first three months of pregnancy, 6,000 mg per day during the second trimester, and 8,000-10,000 per day during the third trimester. Such large doses of vitamin C will help the babies form strong connective tissues.

Since the B-vitamins help prevent birth defects, and since most babies are vitamin D deficient even when their mothers take prenatal vitamins, since we know that vitamin C helps form the skin and strong connective tissues, and since almost everyone is mineral deficient in their diet, every woman who wants a healthy baby should be taking mega-vitamins *before and during* pregnancy as recommended by their doctor. This is paramount.

She should also favor a diet that includes bone broth soups, cod liver oil, olive oil, fresh foods, organ meats, fermented and sprouted foods, green and red vegetable powders (Superfood drinks) and mineral supplements such as Shilajit. She should especially take pains to avoid sugar and vegetable oils!

Eating the right foods and supplements will have long-lasting beneficial effects for the developing child. When a woman eats right during pregnancy she will beget children whose facial features are more symmetrical and beautiful. For this to happen it is also important that women *space out their pregnancies* so that they have time to recover from the nutrient drawdowns they have experienced from the last one.

In *Deep Nutrition*, Catherine Shanahan MD and Luke Shanahan reported that if you want your children to be extremely healthy, intelligent, able to excel at sports and *so physically beautiful that they are striking* then an expectant mother should be eating a surplus of complex, nutrient-dense nutrition that avoids sugar and vegetable oils, as stated.

She should avoid sugar, corn and soybean oil, eat nutrient-dense foods, and take ample (vitamin-mineral) supplements to avoid nutrient depletion in order to produce a baby with the best bone growth and skeletal development including that of the lumbar spine, teeth and jaws, which translates into a more beautiful appearance that includes facial symmetry. If you want to raise an attractive child – *even good-looking enough to be a model* – you must avoid sugar and vegetable oils during pregnancy and eat a nutrient-dense diet! Nutrient-dense foods are nucleotide-rich foods such as liver, sardines, oysters, spirulina, chlorella, mackerel, brewer's yeast and most beans.

The Shanahans found that the most attractive children in a family are typically the oldest. In families of three or more, it is usually one of the first two children because of better maternal nutrition or the fact that the second child benefits from better uterine blood circulation during gestation due to there having been a first child that exercised the womb. In any case, the avoidance of nutrient depletion, which can be countered by the right foods (such as bone broth soups) and supplements, as well as avoidance of sugar and vegetable oils, tends to produce the most favorable looks. It is a great pity that most expectant mothers don't know this.

The Price-Pottenger Foundation offers balanced food guidelines which I subscribe to: eat whole, fresh, unprocessed (non-GMO) natural foods; eat only foods that will spoil; eat naturally raised or wild proteins (fish, chicken, beef, etc.); eat whole (full-fat), naturally produced milk products, preferably raw milk and fermented products such as whole yoghurt, kefir, whole cheese and fresh raw sour cream; use only traditional fats and oils (butter, animal fats, extra virgin olive oil, expeller pressed sesame and flax oil, coconut oil, palm kernel oil and palm oil); take cod liver oil regularly to supply your body with vitamin A and D; eat fresh fruits and vegetables, preferably organic; eat whole grains and nuts (that have been prepared by soaking, sprouting or sour leavening to begin to neutralize phytic acid and other anti-nutrients); include enzyme-rich lacto-fermented vegetables, fruits, beverages and condiments in your diet on a regular basis; prepare homemade meat stocks from the bones of naturally raised animals; use herb teas; use spring water or filtered water for cooking (and bathing); use unrefined sea salt; use a variety of organic herbs and spices for cooking; use unrefined and natural sweeteners (in only mall amounts); cook in glass, stainless steel, or good quality enamelware.

An aspiring mom who is pregnant needs to avoid frozen, canned, vitamin-poor foods and a generally unhealthy diet to conceive the healthiest and best looking baby. Naturally she should avoid alcohol, drugs, cigarette smoking and other vices as well. If a mom is malnourished because she doesn't eat nutrient-rich foods then it will affect the skeletal structure and features of her coming baby, so she has to eat well, and among other things "eating well" means *avoiding sugar and vegetable oils*.

The demands of producing a baby draw down maternal stores of all sorts of nutrients, so for the best looking babies a mom has to space her children apart to give her body time to recover from the last birth, eat lots of different nutrients, and take vitamin-mineral supplements. Actually, she should start taking supplements even before conception in order to prepare for a coming child.

Another issue regarding children within the womb is whether you can teach them during gestation, and the answer is yes. The music a mother listens to, and her emotions, all affect the growth and personality of the fetus growing inside her. Ask expectant mothers and they'll tell you that their babies often know what's going on. Pregnant women should therefore always listen to inspiring, happy music during their pregnancy. They should personally try to avoid stress, and try to be happy and worry-free because the mother's good thoughts and happy energy will be imprinted upon the fetus.

It is also especially helpful for a woman to recite the sacred prayers of her religion during pregnancy, and especially the literature of her tradition's saints. If you have a household deity, an expectant mother should chant the name, mantra or prayers of their deity with a joyful heart and reverence. This will help to bring in blessings from spiritual beings who will help to look after the growth of the fetus. The key is to cultivate the ever-present emotion of joy that will be passed on to the fetus.

Remember that a mother should avoid alcohol, drugs and other harmful substances that can interfere with the development of a baby's perfect body, for no spiritual powers can override the destruction caused by toxic substances absorbed by a fetus during gestation.

Once you have children the next question is how to raise them. In particular you want to teach young children lessons that will prepare them to create a wonderful life for themselves, and you want those lessons to stick. You want them to become good, virtuous people – independent moral agents secure in their own identity who are able to think for themselves and do what is right rather than wrong. Life offers plenty of choices and you want them to be able to think through options and always take the high road of ethics. You want them to take moral values into consideration when making decisions rather than turn into "errant men of business" who will trample anyone or do anything to make a buck.

You also want them to grow up to be good citizens and good neighbors who can enjoy excellent social bonds with their community, meaning that they can live cooperatively and harmoniously within society. Psychologist Jordan Peterson said that your fundamental job as a parent, especially for a child less than five years old, is to make your child "eminently desirable socially" so that all sorts of other children want to play with him or her when they are four. Being desirable as a playmate means you have taught them to be agreeable without major dislikable behaviors and they have the social skills of getting along with others. It means they are a well-socialized kid.

Lastly you want your children to learn sufficient technical and life skills so that they can make a living. The goals is that they can establish autonomy through an independent living that lets them stand on their own two feet in the world without needing any help from others. The ultimate goal is that they eventually become able to live independent, self-reliant lives of prosperity, peace and harmony without being a burden on you, your family or society.

All children come into this life with personality traits, special skills and particular aptitudes that they accumulated in their past lives, and they all have their individual fates and fortunes. The best you can do for them is to prepare them for the world and help them to find their way, which includes training them and steering them away from bad thinking and influences. You can help them develop what is already great within themselves, and should help them change their negative habit energies or *samskaras* into good ones. This is your karmic responsibility.

One's personality traits, habits, karmic energies, innate dispositions, or *samskaras* are the forces that determine your fate in this life and subsequent lives. We develop them in this life due to our genes, our parents and environment, but also inherit a great deal of our tendencies from previous lives. One of our major jobs as parents is to help our children transform their negative proclivities into positive ones. You have to help them change their errant inherited tendencies into good ones. To encourage children to change themselves in positive directions you must give them role models of behavior, heroes they can look up to and emulate.

There are many different educational theories on teaching children, but I favor those that involve moral lessons and frontloading them with huge amounts of diverse experiences, and stretching their talents and skills at particular ages. Which skills and ages? Those skills connected with certain regions of the brain during the age at which science shows those regions are most developing. In other words, you should teach children particular skills and lessons according to the known stages of brain development. By challenging neurons to build better networks during the times those brain regions are forming you will maximize an individual's chances for greater skills and comfort in those areas of development.

You should always expose children to new experiences in life because this makes their lives far richer. Isn't that something you wish someone had done for you? The result of constantly being exposed to new experiences is that children get used to accepting new things in life, and then can adapt to survive much better than others. Innovation and change, which are the nature of the world, are what propel society forward but a lot of people cannot accept change (newness) and get stifled in their life because of rigidity. You have to teach your children that change is the way of life and they should be willing to change themselves to stay afloat or get ahead. Furthermore, children will feel comfortable with novelties and not shy away from them as they get older if they were taught to embrace them when young. New experiences also develop new regions of the brain, and you never know if those developments could lead to your children's career or calling in life.

It is also particularly important to introduce young children to art, music, and literature that might stimulate feelings of happiness and joy as well as transcendence, sublimity, amazement, awe and wonder that might uplift them, inspire them, and let them taste an experience of mental quiet. Children and adults both need exposure to art, music and dance for inspiration, for helping them to manage their emotions, and so that they can quiet their minds in this busy world. Mental calming or quieting can be accomplished when they see incredible beauty and sublimity, such as when they visit nature. This is another reason that children should often be exposed to the beauties and wonders of nature. Anything that gives rise to feelings of amazement, wonder and awe that quiets mentation rather than just stimulating it is also nutritious fertilizer to a young mind.

The basic personality template of an individual is formed well before their teenage years, so in terms of character formation the most critical time in a child's life is when they are young and can easily absorb influences from their parents and the environment.

Trauma, as well, will leave behind a distortion in their thoughts. During these formative years you should police their environment, what they are exposed to and how they spend their time. You have to present them with high ideals and good role models for all the aspects of their life.

In their early and teenage years you should not expose them to too much junk food and should provide foods that are as much organic and non-GMO as possible while focusing on the Price-Pottenger diet that especially avoids sugar and bad fats such as margarine and vegetable oils. A good diet at this time will establish the physical foundation they will have for the rest of their life. If they eat junk food now it will be incorporated into their cells, and illness will usually appear around twenty years later. You must teach your children the importance and consequences of good nutrition.

In addition to the diet, young children need to stretch and exercise, which bestows grace on the physical form. They need to find the limits of their bodies, and learn how to use their minds to control their energies, muscles and movements. The best types of exercise require coaches who can teach children what to do and what it's all about.

Since the personality template forms in the early years, this is especially the time to emphasize character education, which among other things should emphasize values, virtue, ethics, manners, politeness, demeanor, communication, cooperation and mindset. It is easier to teach the ways of virtue and ethics to children than adults, and it is our karmic job as parents to do this for our children by teaching them moral tales and stories of great heroes who might inspire them as models. As parents we must not leave it entirely to the schools but give our children a very firm foundation in moral training.

In Thomas Jefferson's 1818 Report of the Commissioners for the University of Virginia, the "objects of primary education" included such qualities as, "morals, understanding of duties to neighbors and country, knowledge of rights, and intelligence and faithfulness in social relations." These are all important aspects of character education that you have a parental responsibility to emphasize. Don't expect the schools to do this for you. Once again this is a parental responsibility to focus on your children's character education. They come to you for you to do this!

D.P. Doyle revealed the historical framework for character education when writing that "From the time of the ancient Greek to sometime in the late 19th century, a singular idea obtained: education's larger purpose was to shape character, to make men (and later, women) better people." Parents normally expect the public schools to help their children become both smart and good, which is what Socrates defined as education, but it is actually *your* job to emphasize goodness at home and you should also assist in the smart agenda as well. Education asks children to change in directions chosen by adults, and you must choose those directions and foster development along those lines.

You must, for instance, teach your children to tell the truth (honesty), or at least don't lie, and certainly don't steal. You can come up with all sorts of reasons why human beings should tell the truth and not steal other than just the Golden Rule of reciprocity (don't do to others what you wouldn't want done to yourself). The bottom line is that personal integrity as a character trait is the bedrock of successful, trustworthy relationships and leads to happiness, flourishing, fulfillment and well-being.

You should teach children the basics of the Ten Commandments or your religious equivalent, and the fundamental ethical rules that seem universal because they are found in nearly every religion. For instance, most every religion includes some version of the Golden Rule that prohibits people from abusing others, namely forbidding them to do to others what they wouldn't want done to themselves. Only the irreproachable line of conduct should alone be acceptable in life, and that is the pathway of noble, consummate conduct.

There are all sorts of qualities of mind and moral virtues you should also teach your children such as generosity, kindness, fairness, honesty, dignity, self-control, courage, justice, simplicity, moderation, forgiveness, frugality, compassion, patience, resolve, fortitude, politeness, dignity, open-mindedness, appreciation, love of learning, unpretentiousness, friendliness, wisdom etcetera. Every couple, husband and wife, has a different set of values they deem important to pass onto their children based on their own individual experiences, culture, religion, education and upbringing.

Remember Socrates's quote that education has the purpose of making children become both smart and good? Along these lines you should also help your children with their homework, or even go so far as teaching your children lessons on your own that your school may not teach or be good at. Don't leave everything to the schools. My parents, for instance, taught me and my brothers and sisters arithmetic at home, checked our essays and always helped prepare us for spelling bees. They furthered my own education in many other ways too. I became a valedictorian of 1,000 students and all my brothers and sisters did super well academically because my parents got involved and showed concern for our studies, thus letting us know that academics were important. They constantly repeated "do your best" to us but they never criticized us when we didn't do well if we said we did our best. We were taught that we didn't need to know everything or pretend that we did, but we had to exert ourselves to master a body of skills and knowledge and then do our best. Since time immoral, it has always been a parent's responsibility to teach their children both academics, skills, and values at home to some degree. You have a karmic responsibility to not just take care of but to train your children.

In *Buddha Yoga* I listed several special super skills children could also use throughout their life that are not taught at school, and which parents might teach their children if they can. These include the ability to concentrate, do math in their head, size up probabilities, control their inner energy and emotions, and powers such as visualization, mind-mapping and super memory skills. They should also be taught goal setting along with stress and time management skills too.

For instance, the father of famed golfer Tiger Woods taught Tiger how to ignore distractions by making loud sounds, dropping his keys, or doing other bothersome things when Tiger was concentrating on making golfing puts. He did this in order to teach Tiger how to ignore distractions and develop the powers of concentration.

As a parent, one of your jobs is to teach your children skills such as concentration so that they can stick with tasks and challenges in life with unremitting perseverance. You want to help them develop resilience and coping skills, namely grit, which will enable them to accomplish great things in their life. You must prepare them for the future in the ways that schools will not by teaching such lessons.

In particular, you must teach children to take responsibility for how they feel and what internally happens within their own minds. It happens within *them*, so they need to learn how to control it just as they need to learn how to control their impulses and internal energies. I put such lessons in *Color Me Confucius*. Sometimes in life you will get possessed by stupid ideas you cannot control, such as an infatuating attraction to the wrong person, so you need to teach children that stupid ideas happen but they can break their spell and regain control over their minds. Furthermore, as William James taught, the world does not determine how you feel, you do! You must learn how to take charge of your emotions and behaviors, and children need to be taught this skill which is the specialty of training disciplines like NLP, EFT and ACT.

Children need to be taught that happiness is a state of mind that they develop themselves, and not something simply due to conditions. They should be taught that the most precious gift in life is an optimistic, sunny disposition that they can cultivate in themselves. Smiles are free and uplift others as well as yourself. They also need to be taught that everyone creates their own fortune and destiny in life, and therefore they need to take personal responsibility for constructing it.

Children need to be taught that to change their situation in life they must stop avoiding what needs to be done and take the pains to just do it. In order to move ahead they need to chart a course of action and then work towards achieving their goals to get what they want. They don't have to do things the way everyone else does to fit in if they don't want as long as they're not harming others. These are the standard rules of goal setting and achievement that schools don't teach children.

For instance, children need to be taught that successful people are not lucky but are successful because they determine what they want and then do what unsuccessful people are unwilling to do to get it. They don't complain but just do what needs to be done. They need to be taught to avoid self-destructive, self-defeating behaviors such as smoking, drinking, procrastination, laziness, and so on that will prevent them from staying healthy and accomplishing their own personal goals in life. To keep the body in good health is a duty otherwise we shall not be able to keep our mind clear, balanced and string. The lesson is that sometimes you are your own problem, your own barrier to happiness and success in life so you must recognize that you are accountable for your own actions. You are also stronger than your misfortunes so must size up yourself and stop doing stupid, errant things to set your life straight and move ahead.

Children must also be encouraged to become lifelong learners of self-training, and the fact that it is a lifelong necessity to work on their faults, polish their personality, learn new skills and perfect their behavior. It is a lifelong responsibility to train their mind to learn new bodies of knowledge, and master their consciousness. Teach them to watch and improve their thoughts, words and deeds and remember not to believe every stupid thought they have, but to question their thoughts and live in a rational manner.

In Confucianism, this is part of the Great Learning for life. The method for doing this, and how to change your own habits and behavior, is taught by Benjamin Franklin and Yuan Liao Fan which I covered in *Color Me Confucius*. The "immeasurable emotions" methodology of Buddhism for developing new personality traits, taught within *Buddha Yoga*, should also be taught to children as well. You must not only teach your kids to become lifelong learners who adapt to change gracefully, but must also teach them *how to learn*. They must learn how to acquire information because no one will just give it to them.

You must teach your children that their talents and personality are not fixed. Talents can be learned and they can also mold their character like a sculptor can mold a piece of clay. Because personality traits are not set in stone like plaster of Paris, they can cultivate any characteristics they want, and any talents too. You can develop any character traits you want through the methods within *Color Me Confucius* and *Buddha Yoga* just as you can learn any talent or skill you want simply by following Daniel Coyle's road of deep and deliberate practice.

History teaches that George Washington, Theodore Roosevelt, Dwight Eisenhower, Benjamin Franklin and George Marshall didn't particularly like their own temperaments and character traits, which they each saw as an impediment to success, so each one subjected himself to a pathway of self-development in order to drop errant ways and develop new virtues. They became great men because they worked on transforming their personalities and behaviors, such as controlling anger, and the methods they used I put in *Color Me Confucius*, *Buddha Yoga* and *The American Reader*.

Children aren't the only ones who need these lessons. You too have the ability to mold your character to become whatever you choose to be in life. You and your partner can form an ideal image of what you want to develop in your marriage and then take steps to produce that vision. You can chase after any ideals you desire. You will not be the same person thirty years from now, for sure, but you can actually develop yourself to become whatever you want rather than just let undirected change happen to you. You can work on developing your marriage in certain ways too.

What is it that you personally want to become? Start working on creating *that* self just as an actor creates a persona, such as when Archibald Leach turned himself into Cary Grant. Children need to be taught this capability of self-development and how to change themselves to go in the direction they want.

There are many lessons you might teach young children so that they develop useful personality traits and skills. Richard Feynman's father taught him to be curious enough to want to figure things out, and he said that it was this curiosity that led him to becoming a Nobel Prize Winning physicist. His father brought out his curiosity through a variety of ways that created a burning passion inside him, and he has credited his father with helping him become a great scientist because of this. The members of the music group, the Jackson Five, also commonly credit their father for making them the musicians they became.

Some parents might want their children to develop athletic skills because of what sports gave to their own lives, so they encourage them on the road of athletics. Active children interested in sports or dance want to learn how to move their bodies and master their energies through those skills. Some parents focus on passing on the lessons of hard work and perseverance (you get what you work for, not what you wish for), or other lessons that involve key traits for successful lives. Grit and perseverance, which you can also think of as commitment or concentration, help people stay with the goal of accomplishing something despite any obstacles that arise. Along these lines, complimenting children on their hard work and effort is more important than applauding their results because results can never be guaranteed in life but you can certainly instill within children the success habits of hard work and perseverance. When children say they cannot do something or master a task you have to teach them that the right attitude is "not yet." Reward them for practice, not necessarily for results.

As a parent you should try to instill within your children a degree of self-confidence so that they expect to succeed, teach resilience so they keep trying if they haven't yet succeeded, and help them develop coping skills to control their fears and emotions when times get rough. You should encourage them to take risks to change things to move ahead and not to be stopped by fear or overwhelmed by what they deem are the challenges they see. Entrepreneurship, for instance, is a matter of taking risks. Therefore, mastering a new skill or overcoming negative circumstances is not something that will never happen. They need to be taught that they are always in the present here and now state of "not yet" that will change over time with their continually applied efforts. Even marriages grow better through consistently applied positive behaviors that become *consistent habitual behaviors*. Aside from grit and perseverance as attitudes for success, two of the most commonly cited values that parents also want children to develop are kindness and empathy for life in general.

Some smart parents try to cure their children of the desire to be approved by others and instead teach them to listen to their inner self about what is right or wrong. They tell them to simply do a good job in whatever they do without seeking public approval. These can become great leaders in their fields because these children develop strong moral fiber in sticking to what is right despite external criticism and naysayers in the crowd.

Along these lines, parents should teach their children to always follow their heart and be their own authentic selves rather than conformist drones pursuing financial success. Otherwise they'll end up doing what they don't like or know is wrong because of money and then despise themselves and hate their life in the process. Many people end up living bitter, deceitful, arrogant or vengeful lives because they have pursued the outer trappings of money, power and success through wayward paths, and inwardly hate themselves because they cannot justify that mode of being despite their confident outward appearance. Children need to hear this lesson. They need to become authentic to their own beliefs and actualize the best versions of themselves, elevating themselves to some exceptional purpose or source of positivity they want to be.

You must teach them, "Will you enjoy yourself in life or hate your life if you are just chasing the almighty dollar?" Children need to learn that if you don't choose a noble pathway throughout life and pursue things that excite, motivate or inspire you then you'll usually become bitter, unhappy or ultimately unsuccessful in the end. Warren Buffett aptly advised us to tell young people to "look for the job you'd take if you didn't need a job because that's the one that excites you and your passion."

Children need to be taught that fortune in life

comes and goes like the wind in unpredictable ways we cannot control. That is why ancients invented astrology to forewarn us of forthcoming affairs. There are definitely times you'll rise and times you will fall, therefore simply pursuing money/success by abandoning the rules of morality and justice is a sure strategy for eventual misery since it cannot guarantee those results anyway but will certainly guarantee future remorse and regret in the end. Disaster can take away everything you have ever worked to achieve, and then what do you have? What was it all worth to gain money and then lose yourself? It is not worth the price of not being noble and enjoying inner fulfillment and peace of mind in return.

Some parents want to teach their children the valuable skill of listening to others because people tend to talk too much in life rather than listen. Listening is the basis of good relationships, especially marriage. You should cultivate a bit of humility in life to collect the opinions of others, always assuming that the person you are listening to might know something that you don't. As any good doctor will tell you, you learn from others by being quiet and listening to what they have to say. Then you can speak. Life isn't about being right all the time but about learning, and you learn by listening. This isn't taught at schools so parents should make an effort to teach their children strong listening skills. Listening skills, and responding with kindness, will help with your marriage too.

In some cultures the parents try to emphasize the

importance of cultivating interpersonal skills and relationships, especially strong friendships. Marriages themselves should start from friendships and develop into meaningful relationships, so the ability to form friendships is a lesson to emphasize for they emotionally enrich our lives. The connections of friendships can take you to higher places in life too.

People experience happiness in life from associating with people they like, namely friends. Friends are people who want the best for you, whom you can count on when in trouble because they will actively help you, and who give you the courage to do things simply because they exist. It is the quality of your close relationships that produces true happiness in life, not their quantity, and warm friendships are a big part of that equation. Even spouses should encourage each other to give themselves some private "me" time and also spend some personal time with their friends. Do that because you shouldn't completely lose your own identity in a marriage and should never be stingy on self-care. Give yourself some "me" time in various ways.

Intimacy with the family certainly contributes to feelings of happiness, love and belonging, but family can only go so far in helping you once you encounter difficulties in life. At times you will need to rely on friends to help you when you are in need or in difficulty, especially when you are in locations where you don't have any family. Children should always be urged to create strong friendships in their life. Friends are lifetime relationships who might save you when your encounter negative situations.

Cultivating friendships and getting along with others is important, but parents should teach children that their family is still their basic foundation because the family is what took care of them, gave them unconditional love, and protected and guided them as they grew up. Teach them they have that same responsibility to take care of others. The family should always be taught to be their primary bond and source of strength. Nevertheless, you cannot do all things alone in life, so it is also important to cultivate friends and find the right spouse with whom you are compatible.

As parents you need to show your children lots of love, and especially the love of the family. A mom and dad must show unconditional love, affection and acceptance to their children as they grow up while supporting, guiding and defending them as needed. This is how the feelings of love and belonging grow in a person's heart. In fact, many marriages last even despite large flaws (such as betrayals or infidelities) for the simple reason that the spouses are reliable and dependable in caring for and tending to one another so the partners can count on each other during times of need. The husband and wife are there for each other and follow through on what needs to be done. Each one steps up to care for the other and make them feel protected when it really matters.

The unity of a family, such as is seen when

everyone eats dinner together, is what keeps a family together through thick and thin. Everyone wants this sense of togetherness and belonging in their life, so you must take pains to demonstrate to your children that this is the right way to live and make it happen by conducting many family activities together.

The Ten Commandments are one of the best foundations for character education and it's common sense that if children follow these rules (or equivalent codes of conduct) it will help to keep them out of trouble. Christianity and Judaism use the Ten Commandments for guidance, Buddhism uses the Ten Wholesome Actions and the Eightfold Path, Moslems look to the Koran and Sharia for ethical guidance, and Hindu ethics are to be found in the Vedas and Upanishads. Every spiritual tradition has ethical lessons. While they may emphasize different values, the commonalities of not to lie, steal, kill, commit adultery, harm others and so forth are found everywhere.

How do you make sure your children never go to jail? By teaching them the spiritual lessons of proper behavior found within such sources. You must teach your children to live a life of integrity that involves boundaries, and that it is never okay to violate those boundaries "just this once." As with smoking, lying or taking drugs, "just this once" becomes twice, then three times and then a character of permissiveness is formed that lands children in terrible trouble. A good life or bad life all starts with the passing on of wisdom and character education or the lack thereof. If you don't teach your children that there are paths they shouldn't take then they will most likely flirt with them or even embrace them.

Part of a parent's job is preventing your children from associating with bad influences so make sure that virtue, rather than vice, takes root in their psyche and behavior. It is said that one bad apple can spoil a barrel of good ones, and therefore you must keep an eye on whom your children play and associate with, what they watch on television, what they do on the internet, and what they are taught at school.

In ancient times people entertained themselves through drinking alcohol, drugs, gambling, sex, and (watching) fighting, all of which are vices that can destroy lives when in excess. Today we might add excessive cellphone and internet usage as well as pornography addictions. Your job is to police your children so that they do not fall into these vices, or the new ones destined to come along, and avoid character traits and habits that will end up destroying them through some unforeseen means.

Basically, you shouldn't let children do things in the field of misbehaving that will make you dislike them. Stop them when you see they are doing something wrong, and teach them that errant behavior is improper. Character education is all about respect for oneself and others, ethics and good manners, self-reliance and responsibility, and civic contribution. You help to nurture their well-being and family harmony by also emphasizing good manners, patience, tolerance, and self-control (discipline). Good behavior entails not doing to others what you wouldn't want done to you, such as bullying, so it means not aggressing in any way upon another person or their property. This also means you shouldn't cheat or deceive others either. Don't treat others in any way you don't want to be treated yourself. We can and should read moral tales to children in order to instill these and other virtues in their character, helping them to take hold.

John Wesley said that as individuals we should, "Do all the good you can, in all the ways you can, in every place you can, at all the times you can, with all the zeal you can, to all the people you can, as long as ever you can." Buddhism says we should, "Do all the good you can, cut off any evil when you encounter it, don't block any unborn good from being born, and never let any unborn evil to arise." Teaching this is up to you or not.

Nineteenth-century textbooks were clear on promoting civic virtues to children and taught thrift, honesty and hard work, love of one's country, love of God, and the fact that children have a duty to their parents. In the past, American schoolbooks were actually meant to train a child's character and instill characteristics that would encourage youngsters to support the accumulation of property, the certainty of progress, and the perfection of the United States. This actually set the stage for the economic growth of the country that would, in turn, bring prosperity to everyone as a whole. They were a type of social engineering, but for positive results unlike those revealed by Aaron Russo, Charlotte Thompson Iserbyt and Yuri Alexander Bezmenov that are meant to weaken and destroy a nation.

On this note it is important to teach children about personal economics, namely that they need to become financially responsible and accountable for their future. *Rich Dad, Poor Dad* is a useful book along these lines as are many others mentioned in *Buddha Yoga*. Children need to be taught that no one owes them anything, especially the government, and debt is to be eschewed if they want to get ahead in life. Debt is the one big danger threatening all that can turn most everyone into a prisoner for life. It is okay to live below your means but to be shackled with debt can be deadly.

Along these lines, the Puritan virtues of thrift, savings and hard work championed by Benjamin Franklin serve everyone to good stead and are what built America. As stated, when they become older children can be introduced to more complicated financial concepts such as the explanation of assets and liabilities revealed within *Rich Dad, Poor Dad*. I actually wrote *Super Investing, Move Forward, Quick Fast Done*, and many other books with the primary intent of passing many similar good lessons onto children.

Other than skills and talents they may use for life, in particular you also want to pass on the right *samskaras* to your children. *Samskaras* are a set of values, principles, habits and practices that we inherit from our family, society, culture, religion and nation. They are values, virtues and ways of doing things and thinking about the world that are supposed to make life easier and better, and help you decide between right and wrong.

Our *samskaras* are, in effect, the essence of all the good (or bad) that we have been taught, learnt from experience, and adopted within ourselves as a mindset, behavior or habit. We usually learn them by copying others. However, a child also takes birth carrying the *samskaras* of many previous lives with him or her, which manifest as their personality. You absorb some from your parents, culture and environment and bring some with you into this incarnation.

This is why twins have different personalities even though they have the same genes and are raised in the same environment. *Samskaras* manifest in you as innate dispositions, inclinations, proclivities, habit tendencies, personality traits and karmic impulses. Part of your job as a parent is to help change the bad ones your children possess into good ones.

Since *samskaras* are psychological imprints, creating excellent *samskaras* means inculcating good habits in your children and helping them to eliminate their bad ones. Imprinting children with particular *samskaras* is a way of passing on your own life lessons of behavior, knowledge and wisdom. For example, children will copy the way parents interact with each other and adopt these methods as a *samskara* or pattern they will duplicate. Also, the attitudes of a child toward his parents (and to a lesser degree toward his brothers and sisters) become the "prototypes" of his attitudes toward all the people he or she subsequently meets. For instance, if you teach children the Golden Rule, which is to always treat others as you would have others treat you, they will tend to treat others fairly. However, because they model themselves on *you* they must see this in your own life for this type of lesson to take the firmest hold.

One lesson I sometimes emphasize is that parents teach their children that they should use their mind to enrich their actions with good thoughts and emotions so that those activities naturally become impregnated with good *samskaras*. For instance, when eating food children should be taught to add the emotion of being thankful and grateful during the activity and not just when saying prayers beforehand. When brushing their teeth they need not do it mindlessly but can inject the idea of having bright smiles that pass joy onto others into the action. When reporting to seniors they need to feel the act of being respectful. The point is to teach them how to forgo acting mindlessly by impregnating all activities with a sense of presence awareness and positive emotions. Naturally everyone would have more powerful and accurate speech if they applied this to their speaking too.

When children see someone being bullied they should be taught to stand up against social injustice as Sikhs do. They need to be taught to think of friendship, kindness and compassion in viewing the world so that they are emotionally strong enough to speak up and help a victim in need despite any fear of being bullied in turn. This is a difficult lesson, which is why I say that they shouldn't just think these things but feel any injustice deeply inside enough for those thoughts to affect their energy and provoke a response. It is as if you want your thoughts and emotions to make an imprint on your internal energy so that the feeling is strong enough to impel you to act. Thus the world gets better.

Samskaras are required to make thoughts and actions benevolent. As a parent you must determine what *samskaras* you want to pass on to your children through teachings and which ones you will pass on through the example of being a role model. In truth, values cannot just be taught to children intellectually but must be modeled by the parents and picked up in this way. Boys learn how to behave as men from copying fathers, and girls learn how to behave by copying their mothers. For instance, without any formal instruction a boy learns how to behave by observing how his fathers speaks, holds himself and handles situations.

Parents and relatives imprint behaviors on

children, so in the best of worlds you would want them to see impeccable, consummate behavior on your part. Furthermore, your children must see those values and virtues all around them in the environment. When seeking a new home, most moms and dads worry about the environment because of its possible influence on their children, and this is a reflection of the proper mindset of concern.

Every culture places an emphasis on different values as premier such as generosity, kindness, empathy, honesty, hard work, responsibility, gratitude, respect and so on. These values and virtues build the nation you are in, and it is up to parents to see that their children live in an environment which models these values. You want your children to see the best virtues and values in the social environment around them, and you want to model them for your children as well so that they can see them being demonstrated in your life. Basically, the best type of social conditioning for children is to let them constantly see positive human functioning and flourishing all around them. If those factors aren't in the local environment then take your children to where they can regularly see them and make pains to point out those lessons.

Parents should spend their lives purposefully modeling virtues and values for their children to inherit, who will definitely copy what they see in their parents' behaviors. This type of perfuming influence will affect their natural disposition that they carry over from past lives as a karmic inheritance, and will influence their genetic predispositions that they have inherited due to the genes you have given them. However, genes only account for about 30% to 60% of the variability in people's personalities while much of the rest reflects the impact of the environment in which they are raised as well as what they personally experience in life. Therefore you must take pains to see that your parental role modeling and training ("parenting" or "nurturing") and the environment surrounding your children ("culture") is best for their development.

As individuals we become different from one another because of habituation to our environment. We get used to what we see around us, and if we are sufficiently young we take what we see as being normal and natural unless we are taught otherwise. This is one of the ways in which we adopt habits and values and develop our *samskaras*. Habituation means absorbing and getting used to the influences of our culture, environment, family and education, and then taking these ways of being as normal. Those imprints then become inclinations and tendencies, namely our *samskaras*.

This is why it is very important to read children morality tales and give them examples of moral heroes that they might not normally see on a daily basis. This is so that they develop the right type of aspirations from being inspired by noble behavioral models that can help them break out of inferior patterns.

Most of the beliefs we personally hold dear are not based on any reality at all but have been absorbed from our environment since we were young. They are based on information we have absorbed from society, our parents, and from a whole variety of sources. The degree to which we accept them, even if they are untrue, changes us. This is why religious teachings and morality tales help to elevate society. They instill certain beliefs that establish the norms of ethical, virtuous behavior. Because religion produces such a positive influence, it is very important that children be introduced to the moral ideals of religion when they are very young.

Remember that most *samskaras* are transferred through example, like modeling a bad posture, so it is your parental duty to be conscious of what you are teaching your children by your own behavior. It is also your duty to furnish the right explanations to children for whatever they see. For instance, it is hard for young children to understand intent. If a dad promises to take a boy to a baseball game on Sunday but then must cancel the date when he finds out that they had scheduled some other appointment that cannot be broken, the child may get upset. By an adult's definition dad did not lie, but the boy may feel he was given a false statement.

Any false statement to a child, regardless of intent or belief, is something they usually consider a lie. Therefore you must be careful in providing the right explanations to children for whatever you do so that they don't come to incorrect conclusions and then adopt wrong behaviors. In cases of divorce, for instance, children always worry that it is because of something they themselves have done. You have to correct them of these notions.

Children love to imitate so parents need to monitor themselves constantly to ensure that they provide a good example in their thoughts, words and actions. You must also always let children see other good models of behavior they can copy just as, previously stated, you should expose them to many different experiences in life so that they readily feel comfortable in new environments. You always want to expose their brains to new high-level patterns that will stay with them forever.

Good manners, for instance, are something they should constantly see around them, and so parents need to practice good manners among themselves. In order to develop more consideration, compassion, kindness, empathy and thinking about others' feelings, they should constantly see this around them and then they will develop those traits themselves. If you want your children to be kind, you must demonstrate kindness to them by sharing with others and helping those with less who are in need.

Therefore you must determine what *samskaras* you would really like to inculcate in your children, and determine which ones you are probably instilling without intention so that you can stop providing negative influences. You have to be deliberate about which ones you want to pass on or prevent in order to help prepare them for a better life. Usually you must do this at home because the ethics, virtues, and culture promoted within society are not high enough as a general influence without your extra effort.

The younger their age the easier it is to create positive *samskaras* in children. If you habituate them to doing something every day so that it becomes natural such as brushing their teeth, making their bed, doing chores, showing kindness and doing good deeds for others, respecting parents and guests, being thankful, and so forth, this will become a lifelong character trait and habit practiced with ease.

One particular belief you should never kill within young children, which instills the *samskaras* of hope, aspiration and possibility, is the idea youngsters usually have that they can do anything or become anything in life. I once heard about a study of several hundred world leaders in the areas of sports, the arts, science, business, politics and many other fields. Researchers studied these outperformers to determine what made them so successful and found only one common denominator – their parents never criticized them about their dreams when they were young. Their parents never criticized their children by saying negative things such as, "You can't become a ballerina because you're clumsy," or "You're stupid" or "You'll never get ahead." They always said, "You'll be the best there is."

Basically, these supporting parents never put water on a child's inner fire to kill their imagination. This would have destroyed their aspirations and ideals of self-worth. An interesting fact was that it was usually the parent of the opposite sex who was most supportive and inspiring to the child in encouraging their dreams. They never harmed the child's belief that he or she could accomplish or become whatever he or she wanted, even when it sounded silly such as wanting to become an astronaut. They instilled within them the conviction that they could succeed at whatever they set their minds on doing. They believed in them and supported them, which is the rule you should always adopt for your own children because you never know what they will become in life. Teach your children that they need not conform to others but should be true to their own authentic goals in order to become happy.

Truly, you cannot predict what things your children will ultimately do and what heights they may reach in life. For instance, when you read the biography of Abraham Lincoln you cannot possibly imagine how this illiterate farmhand could ever become President of the United States. A child's fortune is unpredictable as to how high they can go as it all depends upon their belief, willpower and effort.

Therefore, who cares if a child says they want to become a firefighter, singer, astronaut, the President or some other crazy notion. Let them say whatever they want – they are just children so it doesn't matter what comes out of their mouths anyway. The dreams will usually change like the wind – probably as soon as next week! Don't put water on the fire of imagination and aspiration.

Never kill the imaginative stretching of a child. If children grow up thinking there are endless possibilities because you said, "You'll be the best one there is if you work hard" then they will usually work on their dreams and end up living the life they want to experience happiness and fulfillment. Isn't that what you want for your children?

Children don't have to be #1 at any particular thing they do in life because there can only be one #1 in the world. Also, if they aren't the winner they need to take the loss gracefully. They just have to be bold and fearless to do their best, and try to excel wherever and whenever appropriate. In an interview with John Chrichton the advertising legend David Ogilvy once advised people: "Be more ambitious. Don't bunt. Try to hit the ball out of the park every time. Compete with the immortals. Try to make whatever you do the greatest that anyone has ever done. You won't always succeed but reach for the stars. Don't bunt. Be more ambitious. Ambition is the key. Try to do remarkable things. Try to be great. It is the lack of ambition that cripples most people."

Children need to learn that hard work pays, and to get ahead they must often work harder than anyone else. If they can find a job or career or start a business that incorporates their passion then great, but most people are not lucky enough to do this in life.

The real goal is not to be #1 but to be so good at whatever you must do or choose to do that others cannot ignore you, and to be good in the way that externalizes your values and life purpose. Then you can even find meaning in an occupation or situation not to your best liking. Passion will help you succeed.

Life is not just about protoplasmic living but about finding a worthwhile life purpose, making your life count towards something, and not confusing momentary high times and fleeting feelings of happiness (which we certainly at times should pursue) with fulfillment. Children need to be encouraged to find themselves and discover exactly how they wish to shape their life in terms of a stable marriage, family, career, environment and so on so that they can express and accomplish what they want while experiencing an inner sense of peace, serenity, fulfillment and well-being. They have to develop a guide for their life that might be a vision, purpose or inner duty they strongly feel is more than just enjoyment. Teach your children that fulfillment and well-being are not something you magically find but must work at everyday to keep in your job and life, including their eventual marriage.

Money is supposed to bring you more options in life, but children should be taught that it is a fuel rather than destination. Focus on teaching your children that the yardstick of success is *happiness and feeling alive* from doing what they want to do rather than your degree of wealth or income. They must be taught that people have the choice of either living in balance or out of balance with an inner calling but they have to work to find their inner "Why?". Once they find it they can then make decisions that bring it to life. The net result of this set of decisions should be closer to producing a life of wonderful relationships and happiness. You can accumulate a high net worth but if you don't have meaningful relationships then it won't be worthwhile. What is it for and who will you enjoy it with?

On a related note you must also teach children that money will make many aspects of life easier, can buy a higher degree of comfort and open doors to experiences that only money can buy, but money will not buy them happiness, contentment, inner tranquility or fulfillment. People want happiness and well-being in life more than anything else, and you have to teach your children that this is what they must pursue rather than performing soul numbing activities for higher income. They cannot take money with them to the grave and it is supposed to make their lives happier, but you'll find quite a few rich people who are unhappy, miserable human beings. Greedy people also live lives that suck. You cannot have significance in this life if it's all about you and your wealth for you will find joy only in service and sacrifice that makes things better for others. However, while your children must be taught that money will not buy them happiness, lack of money will definitely buy them misery. Therefore you have to encourage them to stay out of debt, refrain from becoming big spenders, learn how to save and invest for the future. I put lots of these lessons in my book *Super Investing*.

Now let's address some other issues. For instance, your posture and demeanor are important throughout life in so many ways. People normally size you up by your posture, and if you learn to sit and stand correctly you typically avoid the back problems that seem to plague people as they get older. Therefore, you must teach your children to stand up straight with their shoulders back and establish other good postural habits. They will then develop a good posture for the rest of their life and naturally be respected for this trait. This seems so inconsequential, but the value of a good posture and demeanor is priceless.

Another important principle: when appropriate be sure to take your children to alternative medical doctors if they get sick, or at least familiarize them with the fact that non-establishment alternatives work and they can be their own healer. In the future this might be the very thing that saves them when traditional medicine fails. They should learn the fact that medical alternatives do exist outside of the mainstream, but they may have to search for them. This includes chiropractic treatments, the AMIT method for fixing muscles, Traditional Chinese

Medicine, vitamins and herbal supplements, homeopathics, bodywork and so on.

By visiting alternative health avenues when young, they will be comfortable with these roads less traveled that might be the very salvation of their health in future years. As a great man once said, "Health is the most precious gain and contentment the greatest wealth," so you must take measures to teach your children how to cultivate these two fortunes and where to go to adjust them when they go astray in their lives. The general principle is to lay a good foundation for your children's physical and mental well-being and let them know how to fix them along avenues that the mainstream does not promote. In life people are seeking financial freedom and security, a high level of health and energy, loving relationships, peace of mind, worthy goals and ideals and feelings of personal fulfillment. You must give your children the skills to purse these aspirations and train them so that they have the foundations for their attainment.

You should also encourage your children to exercise through some type of sports because fitness is the goal and exercise instills grace on the physical form. If appropriate introduce them to dancing, the "soft" martial arts or yoga/Pilates, all of which can establish a foundation for spiritual cultivation later in life should they later choose to follow such a path. If children ever hurt their muscles through an accident, the body tends to shut certain muscles down and switch their load to adjacent ones. Damaged muscles can be switched on again through the AMIT method invented by Dr. Craig Buhler, one of the best kept secrets of world class athletes.

One famous rule in particular: "Don't bother children when they are skateboarding." Children must learn about their body and how to control it by taking physical risks, and you shouldn't interrupt this process. Give theme periods of unbroken time where you don't interrupt their attention or they cannot synthesize the information they are taking in. Give them the opportunity to try and fail, and they'll learn from the experience and be far better for it. Taking physical risks is how children learn courage and control of their bodies. Especially for boys, the act of physically challenging themselves is an essential ingredient for the development of their masculinity. Challenging themselves makes them stronger and wiser, so while you must insure safety you should not interrupt any process where they are in the midst of learning dangerous tasks. Even so, you should always teach children never to risk their health or bodies. Too many people end up dead because of stupid forays into extreme situations where they foolishly risked their bodies for thrills.

A child absolutely needs to learn athletic skills and how to control their body's movements and internal energies. Such talents can indeed be learned but it requires immersion as embodied in the idea of "10,000 hours of practice." See books like *The Talent Code*, *Talent is Overrated* and *Sport Visualization for the*

Elite Athlete for how to teach children to master athletic skills like the Olympic champions do.

Don't sexually confuse young children as to their gender either. Gender is a physical determination, not a mental fantasy others should go along with because you think/feel a certain way at a certain point in time. It is like age in that you may feel a certain age but your biological age is what it is.

At times young boys will have sexual fantasies or dreams where they become girls (which raises their Yin energy), and young girls will sometimes have dreams or sexual fantasies where they become men or grow penises (which raises their Yang energy). This is natural and in no way indicative of gay or lesbian tendencies, or that one should really be or become a member of the opposite sex.

Just let children naturally pass through such things so that they don't stay too long at one stage of development. If it was karma for a child to be born of the opposite sex then it would have happened, so don't encourage sex-changing fantasies when the hormones are developing and giving rise to all sorts of strange emotions and sensations inside their bodies. Some children have chosen to be born into a new gender, and the transition stage might be difficult so don't encourage a regression, especially one involving surgery or hormone supplements. We don't allow children the right to drive, vote, drink or marry until a certain age because of a lack of maturity. We also have age restrictions on nicotine, alcohol and gambling because young minds aren't yet mature/developed enough to make those decisions. Insurance companies don't even lower their rates until individuals are age 25 because that's when they are finally making better decisions, which is a function of the neurology of their brains. Therefore we shouldn't expose young children to undue manipulations of thoughts about being an opposite gender nor allow them to choose permanent life-altering surgery or hormone treatments during the years when they are intellectually immature, emotionally immature and sometimes just plain confused because they are still in the stage of growing up.

Children pass through all sorts of stages when growing up, and we all pass through many strange and foolish notions during life. We develop and then drop many different habits or aspirations to do this or that thing, eat this or that food, dress this or that way, and even pursue this or that job and career. As a wise parent you should understand that such things usually pass like the wind, but don't let children *permanently damage* their bodies, reputations or future prospects. Let young boys be boys and young girls be girls as determined by their genetics, and leave mental gender confusion out of the equation.

There are so many possible lessons to teach children that one cannot mention them all. However, another lesson you should definitely teach young ones is the discipline of self-control and delayed gratification. This is a lesson whose importance was made famous by the Stanford marshmallow experiment where a child was given a choice between a small reward now or two small rewards if they waited for fifteen minutes without giving into the temptation to eat a treat placed in front of them. The treat/reward was often a marshmallow, Oreo cookie or pretzel stick. When left in a room by themselves, with the treat on the table, only a minority of children ate the marshmallow immediately.

In follow-up studies, children who demonstrated patience and willpower by delaying their gratification were found to be more competent, and had higher SAT scores than others. Today the original study participants are in their 40s and 50s. The children who were better at delaying gratification have been found to excel in education, have a greater sense of self-worth, manage their stress better, and are less prone to drug abuse. Delayed gratification played a significant and intricate role in shaping their health, well-being and success.

If you can master patience and self-control to resist temptation by delaying gratification, you will have one of the greatest habits for success in life. You'll be better at saying "no" to the strange and even perverse desires that arise in everyone's mind now and then. Rejecting immediate gratification of desires is often called one of the key personality traits of rich people because the wealthy exhibit a strong ability to sacrifice in the present for a big return in the future. Conscientiousness and integrity are also long-term predictors of success too.

The road of constant self-education (investing in your own self-development), such as by becoming a lifelong learner who reads books, is another habit of the wealthy known to lead to success. James Altucher once said, "You're not going to get rich buying stocks. Put the money into reading, writing, learning, starting your own business. Investing in yourself is by far the best investment you can make." Andrew Carnegies gave essentially the same advice, which is to become a self-learner and invest in yourself to become successful. Robert Kiyosaki (*Rich Dad, Poor Dad*) also said that personal development and self-improvement, and the money spent on it, is always a wise investment. However, children need to see this fact and be told about this avenue, for usually their only exposure to education is schooling. They should see parents or relatives doing things outside of formal schooling to pick up this success trait as a natural habit. For example, in my own family all six of us children saw my mother reading books every evening and my father on the weekend, and we all then naturally took up reading as a habit due to their example and encouragement.

Chores such as emptying the trash or making your bed are also good for children. Chores teach children responsibility and the fact that nothing in life comes for free. Never be afraid to give your children chores.

In fact, you definitely *should* establish chores for your children and make them earn allowances because it is an important part of building character which teaches the necessity for contribution, work and responsibility.

Additionally, if you must apply discipline to your children then use the minimum necessary force, and parents should work in pairs on this matter. It is okay to demand family members to "be better" so don't let infractions slide by because you don't want to impose discipline. Instead, you must insist on a code of behavior within the family. Any discipline should be administered fairly, for children need to learn justice in the world. They also need to learn to make amends for wrongs they have committed.

In *Nurture Shock*, Po Bronson and Ashley Merryman revealed this surprising fact about teen misbehavior or rebellion: "Kids who go wild and get in trouble mostly have parents who don't set rules or standards. Their parents are loving and accepting no matter what the kids do. But the kids take the lack of rules as a sign their parents don't actually care – that their parent doesn't really want this job of being the parent. ...

"Ironically, the type of parents who are actually most consistent in enforcing rules are the same parents who are most warm and have the most conversations with their kids."[8]

Along these lines, it helps to have but to limit the rules for children. Most rules-heavy parents don't actually enforce them because it's too much work, and this causes problems rather than solves them. Remember that when children argue about the rules *it's because they want to follow them*, not because they are rebellious and disobedient! To an adolescent, arguing is the opposite of lying.

Arguing over rules is usually an argument over the restrictions, and not about the authority of parents to set them. Arguing from children is therefore often a form of trying to be honest – a sign of respect rather than disrespect even though most people would think it means the opposite. An errant child would just keep pretending to go along with their parents' wishes and then break their rules secretly whereas the one who makes the noise of arguing is doing so because they want to comply with you.

Parents always forget this fact. They also don't realize that children lie all the time, sometimes to protect themselves or to protect their relationship with their parents. Even adults lie, but you don't want children to adopt this trait as a habit. If they see you constantly lying or shading the truth then they will do so as well.

---

[8] *Nurture Shock*, Po Bronson & Ashley Merryman, (Twelve, New York, 2009), pp. 139-140.

Coming to our final topics on what to teach your children, I always tell parents to encourage their children to read several special books that I believe will help their lives: *Liao Fan's Four Lessons, The Autobiography of Benjamin Franklin, Think and Grow Rich, How to Win Friends and Influence People, The 7 Habits of Highly Effective People, The Wealthiest Man in Babylon, As a Man Thinketh, The Power of Habit, Color Me Confucius, Move Forward, Quick Fast Done, Plutarch's Lives of the Noble Greeks and Romans, Rich Dad Poor Dad, Super Investing* and *The Talent Code*.

Within this list are several books I personally wrote with young people in mind, such as for introducing the daily and weekly introspection methods of Benjamin Franklin and many other great successes in life. The purpose of writing all these books was to pass all my insights on certain topics to the next generation of sufficient age, which is especially why I wrote *Visualization Power, Sport Visualization for the Elite Athlete, Move Forward, Super Investing, Color Me Confucius, Buddha Yoga* and *Quick, Fast, Done*. For the young adult I wrote *Culture, Country, City, Company, Person, Purpose, Passion, World* and *The American Reader*. If they read them, try to discuss these books with your children and press them to tell you what they have learned. If interested in a larger reading list, I've given some ideas for the principles to learn and best books to read for various topics in *Buddha Yoga*, which also talks about what to teach children.

When it comes time for your children to enter the upper grades the big lesson you should keep in mind is what award winning educator John Taylor Gatto, former New York State Teacher of the Year, discovered after many years of research.

Gatto made a study of what the top elite prep schools were teaching in the nation and found fourteen themes in elite education that were missing from the public schools. These are themes that you therefore must teach your older children yourself, instead of the idea that your value is your letter grade, if you want to do your best in preparing them for worldly success. Here are the fourteen themes:

1. A theory of human nature (as embodied in history, philosophy, theology, literature and law).
2. Skill in the active literacies (writing, public speaking).
3. Insight into the major institutional forms of the country (the government structure, courts, corporations, military, education).
4. Repeated exercises in the forms of good manners and politeness based on the truth that politeness and civility are the foundation of all future relationships, all future alliances, and access to places that you might want to go.
5. The ability to do independent work.
6. Energetic physical sports are not a luxury, or

a way to "blow off steam," but the only way to confer grace on the human presence, which can later on translate into power and money. Sports are a type of social play where children learn a proper level of aggression during competition but without any intent to hurt other people. Also, because people can get hurt sports helps you practice handling pain and dealing with emergencies.

7. A complete theory of access to any place and any person.
8. Responsibility is an utterly essential part of the curriculum; one should always grab responsibility when it is offered and always deliver more than what is asked for.
9. Arrival at a personal code of standards (in production, behavior and morality or ethics).
10. To have a familiarity with, and to be at ease with, the fine arts; learning cultural capital.
11. The power of accurate observation and recording. For example, you can learn to sharpen your perception by learning how to draw accurately.
12. The ability to deal with challenges of all sorts.
13. A habit of caution in reasoning to conclusions.
14. The constant development and testing of prior judgments: you make judgments, you discriminate value, and then you follow up

> by "keeping an eye" on your predictions to see how far skewed, or how consistent, your predictions are.

As for college and career advice for children, this is a different issue entirely and once again the topics are found in *Buddha Yoga*. However, I really like the books of Michael Masterson along these lines.

All being said and done, many parents want their children to be successful in life, happy, enjoy well-being and to take care of them when they get older. Maybe they will take care of you and maybe they won't. Did you teach your children filial piety and the need to give back to your parents (and society which took care of them) by letting them see you taking care of your own parents (and contributing to the community)? Did you teach them to love their family and others by showing them unconditional love yourself? Did you give them the feeling they were themselves loved and protected and teach them that family came first?

Astrology can foretell of the likely tendencies of your children, but most people will never consult an astrologer for insights about their children's fate, personality and behaviors. Therefore don't count on what you hope for just because that is what you traditionally see around you and you expect your children to do the same. Rather, you can only depend upon one thing, which is the principle that,

> Children are basically past debts.
> Some come to give back to you and some come to collect from you.

Here are the basic principles throughout all these lessons. You have been with your children in previous lives and they come on account of certain purposes. They come to you on account of karma.

Your role as a parent, your karmic obligation is to help prepare them for life by giving them guidance and instruction, teaching them skills, helping them to change their negative habit energies, and helping them to find their way or inner calling. What you can eventually expect from them in return, or as happiness and success in their own lives as well-being, depends entirely upon what you taught them – values, ethics, morals, behaviors, ways of thinking, habits and virtues – so strive to do your best to instill within them very good *samskaras*.

CHAPTER 6
HOW TO STRENGTHEN FAMILY UNITY

Finally, there are two types of bonds we must consider when talking about your karmic family relationships and the goal of maximizing your own happiness in life. There is the marriage bond between the husband and the wife, and the family bond between all the members of the family including your children.

First, how do we make the marriage bond stronger, the marriage better and maximize marital happiness? By consciously establishing regular consistent habits that make marriages work well, and working to minimize whatever factors normally cause marital friction, unhappiness and divorce. This includes the divorce-producing behaviors identified by Dr. Gottman and the subtle forces within society that weaken the marriage bond if we are not careful.

Of the many things one could warn about, couples must particularly remember not to let their bad times destroy the relationship because they must work through things together. They must always remember to talk after arguments, recognize that sacrifices must be made to the marriage bond (not to the other partner), and must stay sexually faithful to their partner because infidelity usually leads to divorce. Both sexes cheat, by the way, and it's just that women tend to do it more intelligently than men. What they want is safety in a partner and the fact that nobody knows.

With the marriage bond taken care of, how do we strengthen the family bond? Even though everyone is there because of karma, how do we make sure that our relationship with our family becomes an enduring source of happiness?

The answer is by regularly, consistently engaging in family unity activities that re-emphasize the family bond, the family's values, and the responsibility of family members to one another. A strong family sticks together because it has developed a sense of being a team. A couple must therefore take pains to forge a strong family identity so that its members become committed to the family as a unit. To do this, the big three factors that family members must cultivate amongst themselves are encouragement and appreciation of one another, and commitment (support) to one another.

Like husbands and wives, family members can show appreciation for one another in various ways. This includes by expressing lots of appropriate affection, treating each other like best friends, praising the accomplishments of each other, gracefully receiving and giving compliments, looking for the positive rather than negative in the relationships, and remembering/celebrating birthdays and special occasions. Appreciation is showing love in small ways every day.

Besides devotion to one another, strong families also cultivate a sense of commitment and loyalty between family members. Family members can become sick or healthy, wealthy or poor, experience suffering or rejoicing, experience failure or success, acceptance or rejection. In all these various phases of life, a family needs to stress loyalty, togetherness and helpfulness during the ups and downs that its members will experience.

For instance, children should be taught to depend upon the family for protection, and to stand by their parents and each other as a united front during times of trouble such as when attacked by bullies and others outside the family. My own mother always told us that if we ever got in trouble then come back to the family because it will protect us and take care of us. Having assurances like this, and then seeing it, is what cements loyalty and unity within a family group.

If a married couple wants their family to become stronger then its members must participate in activities that emphasize the family while also being told "we are a family that has a bond of responsibility to one another." You can accomplish this through regular daily, weekly, monthly and yearly traditions that bring the family members together and unite them in a single activity.

Family traditions (and the retelling of family stories that emphasize the family heritage) help create a sense of identity for the family as a whole, which is one of the reasons you should always celebrate holidays together. The wife/mother is usually the emotional CEO of the family who sets the internal family tone of peace and harmony, so many of these matters usually fall under her responsibility although they should be handled by both parents.

Bill Bonner has written a valuable book, *Family Fortunes*, that doesn't just talk about multigenerational wealth (see my book *Super Investing* for that) but how family members should frequently come together to reaffirm the family and discuss its goals or commitments in life as a unit. A family itself has to set up an ideal or scheme of progression for its growth.

One of the yearly traditions I recommend is for all family members to make a list of their individual goals for the year around December 31 or January 1st, which marks the New Year. You can find more about this procedure in *Quick Fast Done, Color Me Confucius* and *Buddha Yoga*. It is related to the daily practice of self-improvement taught in *Color Me Confucius* where you remember the activities you did during the day, and report them to Heaven at night before going to sleep. In this case the tradition involves making a to-do list of goals you want to accomplish for the year, and to update your life goals at that time.

Come early or mid-Spring, family members should reflect on how far they've already progressed in accomplishing those goals, and *again* write them down on a separate piece of paper. This should include what they want to do for the year, their life, this world and the universe. They should light a small fire, symbolizing all their vital energies that they usually spend on useless activities during the year, and toss that piece of paper into it to report to Heaven and the universe what they have committed to achieving for the year and how they are progressing so far.

By Springtime one will know whether some of the goals they wanted on January 1 are really worthwhile or not, which is why this family ceremony should be done in the Spring when enough time has gone by to show whether any progress has been made along those lines. In fact, knowing that the ceremony is coming up will force you to actually start working on some of those goals and objectives!

Come mid-Autumn, when most of one's goals for the year should have already been accomplished or worked on, the family members should repeat this procedure in a second little fire ceremony that once again has them writing down on paper what they wanted to do during the year, what they are working on doing for their life, and what they want to do for the world and for the universe. What they burn up at this time is the same information, or whatever they have changed, as well as their progress. Then come December 31st they repeat this process of writing down new goals, vows, or commitments for the year ahead and their life.

The activities that families can share to help tighten their bonds include daily meals, daily prayers, movie nights, household responsibilities and family chores. Mealtimes, chores, picnics, vacations, camping, sports, hiking or walking, recreations (including shared jigsaw puzzles, table games, videos), movies, religious services, school activities and special events like holidays and birthdays celebrated together by everyone are all activities that can be done together. My family, as an example, would always eat dinner together and say prayers together before going to bed at night.

A religious orientation, such as devotion to some tradition, holy book or teacher, is also another important component typical of strong families. Most strong families belong to some type of organized religious body such as a church, synagogue, or temple. When family members practice the same religion and attend services together, and when they adopt the same cultural values and traditions this will also help to cement family unity. Yet another bonus to attending faith-based services is that studies show that attending such services four times per month, regardless of the denomination, adds about fourteen years to an average lifespan. The big point is to gather together regularly as a family.

For greater family unity, children also need to see clear family roles being played by their mother and father who as adults must assume responsibility for leading the family. Both mom and dad have a certain role to play in family life and children have a role to play as well.

Within healthy families there is a clear recognition that the parents are in charge and set the rules and activities of the group. Without this vital role played by parents, a family will weaken. As previously taught, an important thing that parents need to recognize is that when children argue with them it is not because they are bad but because they want to be good and follow the rules. If they didn't care what their parents said then they would just keep quiet and do whatever they wanted anyway while hiding it.

The Chinese Confucian tradition has several principles on family unity and responsibility that individuals of every culture can benefit learning about because they give us some food for thought. You can find a discussion on this within *The Chinese Secrets for Success: Five Inspiring Confucian Values*, which contains very helpful ideas.

For instance, Chinese culture emphasizes that children should take care of their parents in old age just as parents took care of children in their youth. As they become elderly, parents can no longer work, have insufficient income and are subject to health problems, all of which may require the assistance of children grown up. Taking care of parents is therefore a commitment to the family that should be stressed and regularly demonstrated to children when they are young. It needs to be drummed into them. Such behavior shows caring for the family.

In terms of relationships, the Chinese also make an effort to develop external friendships outside of the family's sphere of influence, especially those that enrich their lives. Friends cannot only help us but are important for making life emotionally richer as we all have a need for belonging and love that we can only obtain through social connections. All the money in the world is not worth as much as friends. Life will not take care of you just because you have a good academic record, but friends will. Associating with good and generous friends forms the basis for your moral and mindset development, which is why the Chinese always desire to live in a good community.

The Chinese also stress saving for a better life, while avoiding debt, and managing money conservatively and wisely. Through thousands of years of history that included wars, famines, plagues, floods, economic catastrophes and all sorts of disasters, the Chinese have learned the value of thrift and savings. In today's world we would especially emphasize the principle of avoiding debt for prosperity. *Rich Dad, Poor Dad* also has relevant lessons on financial matters that I wish someone had taught me when I was young.

Within the family the Chinese also stress the importance of education, partly because securing an education was a way to ensure income and status in previous eras of Chinese society. In today's world a higher education can get you a good job and income as a doctor, lawyer, scientist and so on, and thus the security of financial support but not necessarily happiness. Nevertheless, the ideal of pursuing an excellent education exhibits the Chinese ideal of achieving a successful life in a reliable way, and goes hand in hand with the Chinese pursuit of "creating an outstanding life."

In Indian culture the exceptional life involves four aims or goals, which are called *Purushartha* that entails *Kama, Artha, Dharma* and *Moksha*. *Dharma* is ethics, moral values and righteousness, which you are to teach to your children. *Artha* is wealth, prosperity and success or economic values, which you should pursue in a proper degree that isn't above everything else. *Kama* is playfulness, sensual pleasure and love, namely the enjoyment of earthly pleasures in life to generate positive emotions and psychological values. *Moksha* is spiritual liberation, or spiritual values that you should also possess.

With these four aims being proper in life it is therefore important that you *do* give your children a strong ethical foundation, teach them the abilities that will enable them to achieve success and create a better life for themselves, including the ability to control their emotions and generate good ones in place of bad ones. You should also give them a foundation in spiritual cultivation should they choose that road in life. Basically, you need to *train them* in certain ways because that is the proper role of a parent.

When about to pass away, many people lament that they should have traveled more. They also regret that they spent way too much time working instead of having fun with their family and friends. Therefore, for happiness in life always keep your life priorities in mind rather than financial priorities. You have never seen, "He wrote a good business plan" on someone's tombstone. All the money in the world cannot buy a moment of time either.

Remember to make family the priority rather than work, and take adventurous family vacations to expand your horizons and those of your children. Of course, when they are very small an expensive trip to Disneyland is unwarranted since it means virtually nothing to young children who will not remember it. It is in the later years that trips become more useful in helping children grow.

In successful families the family comes first, which is the reason why couples usually marry in the first place; most people marry because they want deep intimacy with another and want to build a family together with that person. Work responsibilities thus come second. When outside pressures (work, for example) threaten to remove "family" from the top priority, the members of successful families take action and make sacrifices as necessary to preserve the family's well-being. The job, work or business comes second. For the strongest families, family always comes #1 and there is even a close relationship between longevity and putting the family ahead of other concerns.

A last bit of note is that successful families are not isolated but are usually connected to the community and wider society in various ways because of various forms of regular interaction. In fact, when Dan Buettner did his famous Blue Zones research on locations where people commonly live to be well past one hundred years old, he found that there was a connection between longevity and social interaction, namely an individual's engagement with the greater community and their sense of being part of a social group. The world's longest-lived people don't just engage with social circles that support healthy behaviors, but stay heavily involved with community activities in their old age. Long life involves keeping family connections strong and community connections strong too.

And now to return to where we started …

Husbands and wives were connected in the past.
Whether for good or bad, those connections
   never fail to meet again.

> Sons and daughters are basically past debts.
> Some come to give back and some come to collect.

A family begins due to a love expressed within a relationship between the spouses, and that love is due to past life connections as well as efforts made in this life that must be continually fostered. The love and togetherness of all the members within a family starts out as a karmic inheritance, but is something you must build in this life too.

While many say that love should be at the heart of the family, there are situations where there is as yet no love at their beginnings, such as in arranged marriages. In those cases each spouse should still work on building a deep level of friendship and respect for the other that will eventually turn into love. Even with deeply romantic love marriages, the spouses must at first struggle to learn how to live with one another and the same certainly goes for arranged marriages. Romance wears off but the need for work in maintaining harmonious unity stays constant.

Love does not happen automatically. Even with past life connections it requires time and effort for love to grow deeper between the spouses. Just as you don't get in shape from going to the gym for one day, building a strong marriage and family takes time and commitment to a consistent course of action – a set of principles/guidelines you follow and the consistent daily practice of behaviors that keep you on track with them.

The strong intimacy, sharing, belonging, and caring seen within families are an expression of love that will grow over time if you make positive efforts. That love is initially possible because of karmic connections between family members, but will grow only through efforts you make in this life to instill wonderful characteristics into your relationships.

When you marry or gain a child, don't just expect the strongest emotional connections to automatically be there. The big lesson is that you have to develop stronger relationships on what is already there from what you build in this life. You must actively work on strengthening the marriage bond and family bonds. For love to grow you have to work at it.

If the connections of the past were good then love will be easy to grow, but if the connections were poor then it requires more effort to grow a deeper love and gratitude for one another. Even with love the ups and downs of life will be a trying test for marriage and family bonds at times, but couples need to persevere at what they want to build. Never forget that the happiness within the marriage and family bonds is a process that requires commitment to some work. The process can require hard work or easy work because of past life connections, but it always requires work just the same. Approach it all with a positive attitude.

Sickness, death, jobs or economically imposed separation and divorce are some of the many factors that can separate spouses. Finding a spouse takes work while keeping the marriage and family strong takes effort. Remember that it always requires work on your part ... commitment to a course of action and regimen of things, such as bonding rituals you repeat over and over again throughout the years. Marriages are built, improve and stay together from the application of consistent positive shared behaviors, such as an emphasis on communication and connection, that become the consistent, habitual behaviors of the spouses. Spouses need to generate feelings of closeness to one another, feelings of safety and security provided by their togetherness as a union, and create the vision of a common identity and shared future in order to last.

The advancement from staying in the game is what brings you joy, happiness and well-being in the long run so marriage and the family life is a journey that requires patience rather than immediate gratification. Just as abundance happens because of well-designed intention followed by well-designed actions regularly taken over and over again until they become consistent habits that replace the unfavorable actions and responses of the past, a great marriage and family life is created out of similar principles. It is based on consistency, not an intensity of feeling high. It is something that requires work on compatibility issues, but also you have to start with the right partner by eliminating those who don't karmically fit in the first place. You have enough karma to marry several individuals in this life, but you need to select the one with the best compatibility *for this life*. Then you have to get the environment and process right and work at keeping it that way and improving it.

My parting advice? "Make it as good as possible for as long as it lasts."

ABOUT THE AUTHOR

You might be interested in other books by the same author:

Sport Visualization for the Elite Athlete
Visualization Power
Quick, Fast, Done
Move Forward
Detox Your Body Quickly and Completely
Look Younger, Live Longer
Super Investing
Breakthrough Strategies of Wall Street Traders
Bankism
The American Reader
Color Me Confucius
Buddha Yoga

www.ingramcontent.com/pod-product-compliance
Lightning Source LLC
Chambersburg PA
CBHW070734020526
44118CB00035B/1330